PROGRESSIVE

Complete
Learn To Play
Saxophone
Manual

by
Peter Gelling

Published by
KOALA MUSIC PUBLICATIONS™

Like us on Facebook
www.facebook.com/LearnToPlayMusic

View our YouTube Channel
www.youtube.com/learntoplaymusiccom

Follow us on Twitter
twitter.com/LTPMusic

Visit our Website
www.learntoplaymusic.com

Contact us via email
info@learntoplaymusic.com

PROGRESSIVE COMPLETE LEARN TO PLAY SAXOPHONE
I.S.B.N. 978 1 86469 259 4
Order Code: 69259
Acknowledgments
Cover Photograph: Phil Martin
Photographs: Phil Martin
Special thanks to Chris Soole for additional solos, as well
as his invaluable suggestions and proof reading.

For more information on this series contact;
Koala Music Publications
email: info@koalamusicpublications.com
or visit our website;
www.koalamusicpublications.com

CONTENTS

CONTENTS CONTINUED

CONTENTS CONTINUED

CONTENTS CONTINUED

INTRODUCTION

Progressive COMPLETE LEARN TO PLAY SAXOPHONE is the ultimate Saxophone manual. It assumes you have no prior knowledge of music, and will take you **from beginner to professional level**. In the course of the book you will learn **all the essential techniques of Sax playing** along with how to read music, how to improvise and how to analyze music and musical forms. By the end of the book you will be ready to play in a band, understand improvisation and be competent in a variety of musical styles.

The book is divided into sections, the first covering basic reading, fingerings and rhythms and an introduction to forms such as the 12 bar Blues. The later sections cover playing in the high register, more complex rhythms, improvisation and explanations of chords, scales and modes. Each new note and technique is introduced separately and all examples sound great and are fun to play. The examples and solos demonstrate a variety of styles including Blues, Jazz, Rock, Fusion and Funk. The accompanying CD contains all the examples in the book so you can play along with them. The book also features a chart listing all fingerings for the saxophone. **All saxophone players should know all of the information contained in this book.**

The best and fastest way to learn is to use this book in conjunction with:
1. Buying sheet music and song books of your favourite recording artists and learning to play their songs. By learning songs, you will begin to build a repertoire and always have something to play in jam sessions.
2. Practicing and playing with other musicians. You will be surprised how good a basic drums/bass /guitar/saxophone or drums/bass/keyboard/saxophone combination can sound even when playing easy music.
3. Learning by listening to your favourite CD's. Start building a collection of albums of players you admire or wish to emulate. Try playing along with one of them for a short time each day. Most of the great saxophone players have learned a lot of their music this way.

Also in the early stages it is helpful to have the guidance of an experienced teacher. This will also help you keep to a schedule and obtain weekly goals. To help you develop a good sense of time it is recommended that you **always** practice with a metronome or drum machine.

USING THE AUDIO

It's recommended that you use the accompanying audio available either on CD or online. The book explains the techniques to use, while the audio lets you hear how each example should sound when played correctly. A disc icon with a number, as shown below, indicates a recorded example available on CD or online (see the front of this book for more details). This book comes with a compact disc that includes all the examples in the book. There are two versions of the CD - one for Alto or Baritone sax (E♭), and one for Tenor or Soprano (B♭). The book shows you the notes, fingerings and techniques, and the recording lets you hear how each example should sound. Practice the examples slowly at first, gradually increasing the tempo. Once you are confident you can play an example evenly without stopping the beat, try playing along with the recording. You will hear a hi-hat cymbal count-in at the beginning of each example, to lead you into the example and to help you keep time. To play along with the CD your saxophone must be in tune with it. To learn how to tune your sax to the CD see page 13. The first track on the CD is the G note used for tuning on page 13. Once you are in tune with this note, you will be able to play along with the CD.

CD Track Number

1. **G Note**

BEFORE YOU BEGIN

SAXOPHONES

There are **four** basic types of saxophones: **Alto**, **Tenor**, **Baritone** and **Soprano**. The two most common are the Tenor and the Alto. Saxophones are fairly expensive to buy new, so you may want to hire one until you are sure you are going to persevere with it. Many music stores have good saxophones to rent, and some also have hire purchase plans. If you are buying a second hand instrument, there are a couple of things to look out for. First make sure there are no dents, bends or cracks in the instrument, as this will affect the tuning. Also check for leakage by playing over the range of the instrument to see whether you can get all the notes to sound properly. If possible, have a professional check out the instrument before you buy it.

REEDS

The reed is attached to the mouthpiece and vibrates to create a sound when you blow. Most reeds are made of cane, although it is possible to buy synthetic reeds. To begin with, you will probably need to use a fairly soft reed such as a 1or 1½. As your lips and facial muscles develop you will be able to play with harder reeds. The higher the number on the reed, the thicker it is, making it harder to play but also producing a stronger tone. The choice of reeds is a fairly personal thing. When selecting a new reed, make sure it has no cracks around the tip and is not warped. These things can make it difficult or impossible to get a good sound. Keep your reed in its plastic cover between practice sessions. This way it will last longer.

APPROACH TO PRACTICE

From the beginning you should set yourself a goal. Many people learn saxophone because of a desire to play like their favourite artist (e.g. Maceo Parker), or to play a certain style of music (e.g. Rock, Blues, Funk, Jazz, etc.). Motivations such as these will help you to persevere through the more difficult sections of work. As your playing develops it will be important to adjust and update your goals.

It is important to have a correct approach to practice. You will benefit more from several short practices (e.g. 15-30 minutes per day) than one or two long sessions per week. This is especially so in the early stages, because of the basic nature of the material being studied and also because your lips and facial muscles are still developing. If you want to become a great player you will obviously have to practice more as time goes on, but it is still better to work on new things a bit at a time. Get one small piece of information and learn it well before going on to the next topic. Make sure each new thing you learn is thoroughly worked into your playing. This way you won't forget it, and you can build on everything you learn. To be sure you develop a good sense of time, **always practice with a metronome**.

In a practice session you should divide your time evenly between the study of new material and the revision of past work. It is a common mistake for semi-advanced students to practice only the pieces they can already play well. Although this is more enjoyable, it is not a very satisfactory method of practice. You should also try to correct mistakes and experiment with new ideas. It is the author's belief that the guidance of an experienced teacher will be an invaluable aid in your progress.

For more books and recordings by Peter Gelling, visit: **www.bentnotes.com**

LESSON ONE

PARTS OF THE SAXOPHONE

Shown below is a photo of a tenor saxophone with the neck separated from the body. These are the two basic parts of the saxophone, apart from the mouthpiece, which fits onto the cork at the top of the neck. All the parts are labelled. Look at the photo and memorize the names of all the parts.

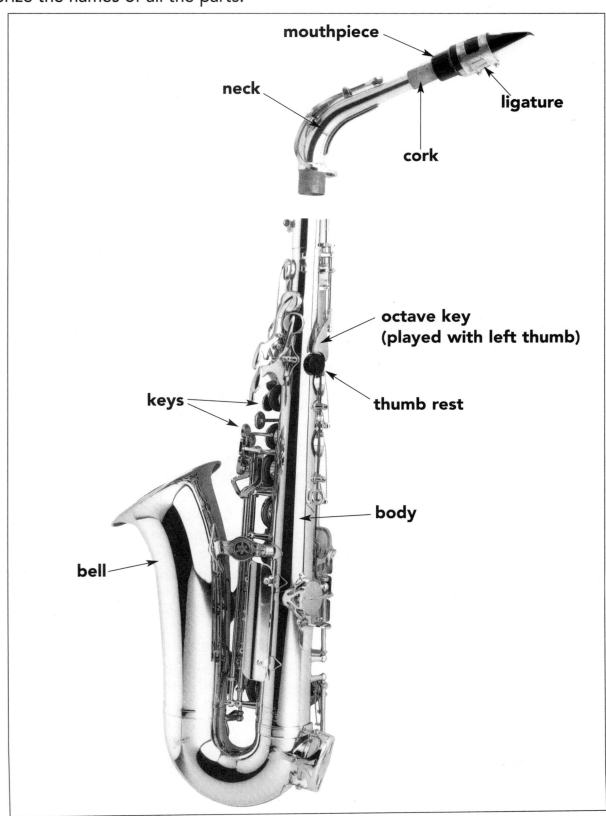

PUTTING THE SAXOPHONE TOGETHER

The saxophone is a relatively simple instrument to assemble, since there are only three basic parts – the body, the neck and the mouthpiece.

ATTACHING THE MOUTHPIECE

A crucial part of the assembly is attaching the mouthpiece to the neck. Notice that the end of the neck has cork around it for the mouthpiece to fit onto. It is important not to damage the cork as it is essential for keeping the joint airtight. When attaching the mouthpiece to the cork, twist the mouthpiece gently as you push it gradually about two thirds to three quarters of the way onto the cork. When you are finished, hold the neck in front of you and make sure the flat part of the mouthpiece with the hole in it is facing **downwards**. This is where the reed fits on the mouthpiece. Since the reed rests against your bottom lip, it is essential that this part of the mouthpiece faces downwards. You may find that the cork is very stiff and difficult to work the mouthpiece onto. If this is the case, you will need a small amount of **cork grease** and the problem should disappear.

ATTACHING THE REED

Before attaching the reed to the mouthpiece, you will need to moisten it in order to make a good sound. A dry reed is not flexible enough to make a consistent tone and may be totally unplayable. Some players like to place the reed in a glass of water before using it, while others prefer to use saliva by putting the thin end of the reed gently in their mouth for a short period.

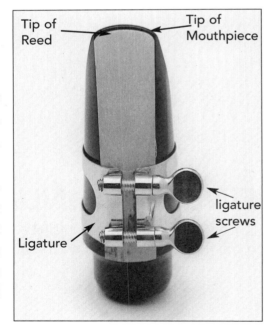

Once the reed has been moistened, slide the flat part of the reed along the flat part of the mouthpiece until only the very tip of the mouthpiece is visible behind the reed. Once you are happy with the position of the reed, hold it with your thumb while you slide the **ligature** loosely into place and then tighten the screws, but not too tight. The ligature holds the reed in place so that it doesn't move when you are playing. To avoid damaging the reed, try not to touch the tip of the reed as you adjust it's position. If the reed is damaged, you will find it difficult or impossible to produce a good sound.

ATTACHING THE NECK TO THE BODY

When attaching the neck to the body, first loosen the screw at the top of the body. use a gentle pressure and twist the neck as you insert it. Line up the mouthpiece with the the left thumb rest and the octave key. Once you are happy with the position of the neck, tighten the screw again, but not too tight.

HOW TO HOLD THE SAXOPHONE

Put the neckstrap loosely around your neck, then attach the neck strap to the ring on the back of the saxophone opposite the bell and adjust the length of the strap so that the mouthpiece is level with your mouth when your head is in relaxed position looking straight ahead of you.

Place your left thumb on the thumb rest near the octave key and place the first three left hand fingers on the keys for the note **G** as shown in the diagram on the following page. Put your right thumb underneath the thumb hook further down the back of the body of the saxophone and then use the right thumb to push the saxophone slightly away from your body (ahead of you) until you are in the position shown in the photo below. This is the basic playing position.

It is important to remember that when you are playing, the neckstrap should take the weight of the instrument rather than your hands, which should be left totally free to control the keys.

FINGERING NUMBERS

The numbers on the fingers show which fingers should be used to press down the keys as shown in the fingering diagram on the following page.

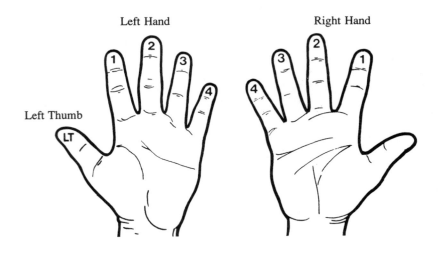

FINGERING DIAGRAM

(These diagrams are used throughout the book)

G NOTE

Left Thumb
The ball of your left thumb should be on this thumb rest when you play. Don't press too hard with your thumb, as you will need it later to play the octave key.

Right Hand Fingers
The right hand does not press down any keys when playing a **G** note. Always keep the tips of your fingers hovering near the keys, ready to play the next note.

Left Hand Fingers
A **white** number on a **black** key tells you to press down the key with the finger indicated. Press down the three black keys indicated on the diagram to play the note **G**.

PLAYING YOUR FIRST NOTE

One of the most important aspects of playing any instrument is the ability to produce a strong, even tone. On the saxophone, this largely depends on the position of the mouth and lips, the amount of pressure used, and the way the air is directed through the instrument. The mouth and lip position is known as the **embouchure**.

To form the basic embouchure for saxophone playing, place the tip of the mouthpiece about one centimetre into your mouth and rest your top teeth against the top of the mouthpiece and bring your bottom lip up against the mouthpiece. You are now ready to play a note. Place your fingers in position for a **G** note and blow a steady stream of air into the saxophone until the note sounds.

Be patient if you cannot make the note sound clearly and evenly at first. Experiment with the pressure from your jaw until you find the right amount to make the note sound correctly. Do not use excessive pressure, and try to let your breath out evenly. As your lips and facial muscles develop, making a good sound will become easier and easier.

Side view of embouchure

Front view of embouchure

TONGUING

To control the beginning and end of a note, the technique of **tonguing** is used. To prepare for this technique whisper the sound **'taa'**. The sound begins with your tongue sitting behind your top teeth, blocking the passage of air, and you make the **'taa'** sound by quickly withdrawing it, and letting a stream of air begin from your outgoing breath.

The next step is to do this with the embouchure in position to play a note, but with your tongue lightly on the reed. As you withdraw your tongue, the note will have a well articulated beginning. To end the note, you put your tongue back on the reed rather than stopping your breath. This will end the note as crisply as it started. It is worth practicing the tonguing technique many times on a single note until you are comfortable with it.

LESSON TWO

TUNING YOUR SAXOPHONE TO THE CD

The first track on the CD contains a **G** note for you to tune to. This is the note shown in the diagram on page 11. The following steps will help you tune to this note. In the beginning you may need help from your teacher, but in time you will find it easy to adjust the pitch of your saxophone to match the CD or other musicians.

To begin tuning to the CD, cue it to the start of the tuning note for your particular saxophone, and then play a G note. Listen carefully to the sound and try to keep it in your mind when you finish playing the note. Then start the CD and see if your note sounds the same as the one you just played. If it does, you are already in tune with the recording.

If your note and the CD note are **not** the same, there are two possibilities. Your instrument may be **sharp** (higher) or **flat** (lower). The pitch of the saxophone can be altered by either pushing the mouthpiece further onto the cork at the end of the neck, or pulling it back a bit.

If you think your G note is lower than the G note on the CD, you can make it higher by pushing the mouthpiece gently a little further onto the cork. Be careful to move the mouthpiece only a small amount at a time, or you may put the instrument out of tune in the opposite direction; i.e. you may make the note sound too sharp instead of too flat. Once you have moved the mouthpiece, play the note again and check it against the CD. Repeat this process until your G note and the CD note sound the same.

If your G note is higher than the recording, you will have to move the mouthpiece in the opposite direction – pulling it back out along the cork a small amount and then checking your note against the CD. Once again, repeat the process if necessary until your G note and the CD note sound the same.

If you have trouble hearing the differences in pitch and matching them evenly, don't worry, this is common and tuning will become easier as your lips and facial muscles develop and you get a better sense of the sounds of notes in general. Many people have to get their teacher to help them tune their instrument for the first few months they are learning. However, it is important to practice tuning to the CD each day, as you will often be required to tune to other instruments when playing with other musicians. Next time you go to hear a band, orchestra or any musical group, notice how the musicians spend a short time tuning their instruments carefully before they begin to play.

HOW TO READ MUSIC

These five lines are called the **staff** or **stave**.

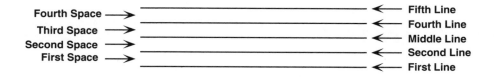

Fourth Space →	← Fifth Line
Third Space →	← Fourth Line
Second Space →	← Middle Line
First Space →	← Second Line
	← First Line

THE TREBLE CLEF

 This symbol is called a **treble clef**. There is a treble clef at the beginning of every line of saxophone music.

THE TREBLE STAFF

A staff with a treble clef written on it is called a **treble staff**.

NAMES OF THE NOTES

There are only seven letters used for notes in music. They are:

A B C D E F G

These notes are known as the **musical alphabet**.
Saxophone music notes are written in the spaces and on the lines of the treble staff.
The **G** note written on the **second** line of the staff is the note you learnt to play on page 11.

To remember the notes on the lines of the treble staff, say:
Every **G**ood **B**oy **D**eserves **F**ruit.

The notes in the spaces of the treble staff spell:
F A C E

NOTE AND REST VALUES

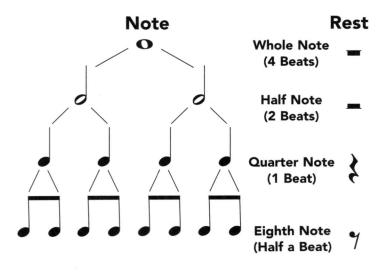

	Note	Rest
Whole Note (4 Beats)	o	▬
Half Note (2 Beats)		▬
Quarter Note (1 Beat)		𝄽
Eighth Note (Half a Beat)		𝄾

Bar lines are drawn across the staff, which divides the music into sections called **Bars** or **Measures**. A **Double bar line** signifies either the end of the music, or the end of an important section of it.

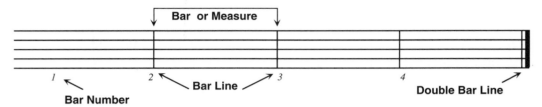

THE FOUR FOUR TIME SIGNATURE

These two numbers are called the **four four time signature.**
They are written after the treble clef.
The ⁴⁄₄ time signature tells you there are **four** beats in each bar.
There are **four** quarter notes in one bar of music in ⁴⁄₄ time.

THE HALF NOTE

Count: **1**   2

This is a **half note**. It has a value of **two** beats.
There are **two** half notes in one bar of ⁴⁄₄ time.

CHORD SYMBOLS

If you look at example 2 on the following page, you will notice two lines of letters and symbols above the staff (B♭ E♭ F7 B♭7 etc.) These are **chord symbols** which indicate the harmony to be played by accompanying instruments such as keyboard or guitar. The **top chord** is for instruments accompanying the **tenor or soprano** sax, while the **bottom chord** is for instruments accompanying the **alto or baritone** sax.

KEEPING TIME

One of the most important aspects of playing any instrument is keeping a strong, even sense of time while you play. This is best developed by counting the rhythms in the music. Before you play example 2, count **1 2 3 4 1 2 3 4** several times to get a feel for the rhythm. As you play the example, count mentally as you play and tap your foot to help you keep time. To be sure you develop a good sense of time right from the beginning, it is recommended that you **always practice with a metronome or drum machine**. Each example on the CD begins with four drum beats. Count along with these beats to help you establish the right tempo (speed) for each example.

WHERE TO BREATHE

When learning any wind instrument, it is important to learn how to take a new breath without losing your timing. To begin with, breath marks will be indicated above the music with this symbol ▼. Take a quick, deep breath from your diaphragm, and be careful not to lose your timing when you breathe. Counting as you play should help you become more confident with this. Breathing technique is discussed in detail on pages 31 to 33.

 2.0

Notice the counting numbers underneath the staff. The bigger **bold** numbers tell you to play a note and the smaller numbers tell you to sustain it until the next note.

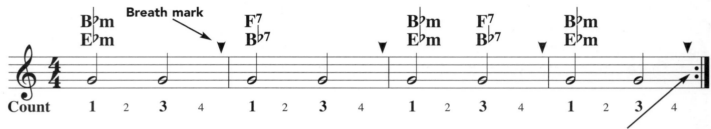

These two dots are called a **repeat sign**. It tells you to play the example again from the start.

THE HALF REST

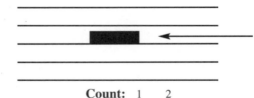

A **rest** indicates a specific period of **silence** in music. The symbol shown here is called a **half rest**. It indicates **two beats** of silence. When you see this rest, count for **two beats** without blowing.

Small counting numbers are used under rests.

 2.1

This example uses half notes along with half rests.

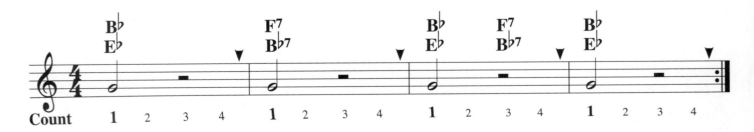

THE QUARTER NOTE

This is a **quarter note**. It lasts for **one** beat. There are four quarter notes in one bar of $\frac{4}{4}$ time.

Count: **1**

 2.2

This example contains both quarter notes and half notes. Don't forget to tongue each note.

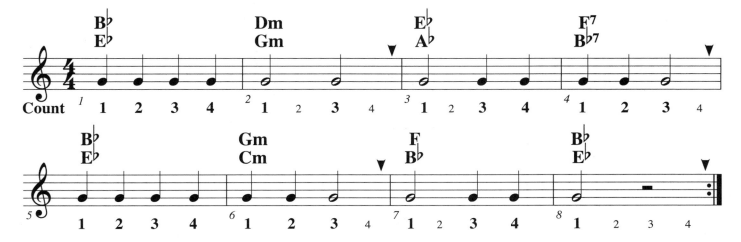

THE QUARTER REST

This symbol is a **quarter rest.** It indicates **one beat of silence**. Do not play any note. Remember that small counting numbers are placed under rests.

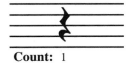

Count: **1**

 2.3

Remember to **count** silently to keep time regardless of whether you are playing a note or a rest.

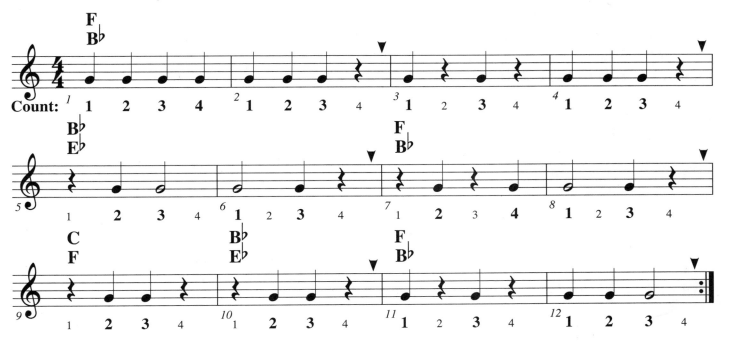

THE NOTE A

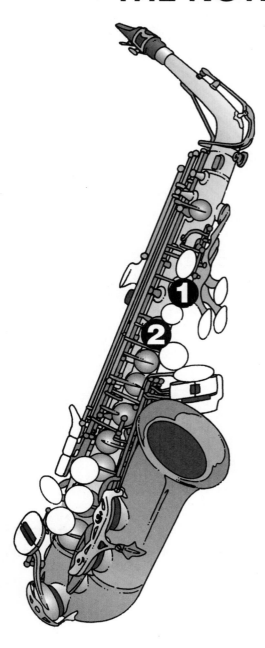

A Note

This **A** note is placed in the **second** space of the staff.

2.4

This example uses the note **A** along with the note **G**. Listen carefully to the notes as you play them and try to produce a **strong, even tone**. Pay attention to the breath marks and get in the habit of breathing each time you see one.

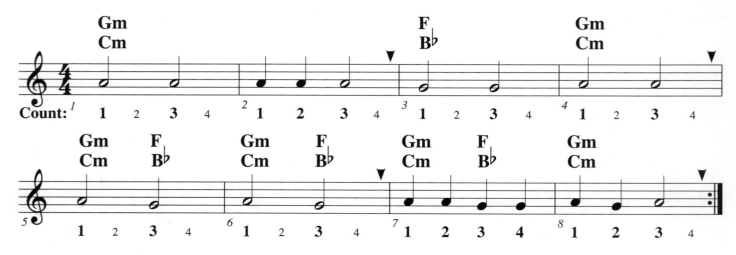

LESSON THREE

THE NOTE B

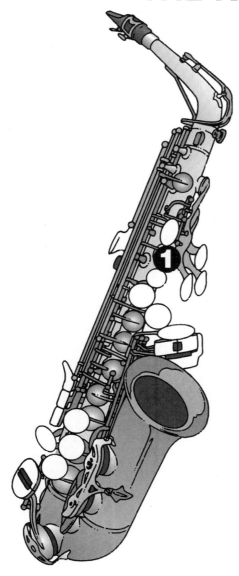

Notes written below the middle line of a staff usually have their stems going **up** on the right side of the note.

The stem for the note **B** may go **up** or **down.**

B Note

This **B** note is placed on the **middle** line of the staff.

 3.0

Notice the two possible directions for the stems of the note **B** in this example. The stem direction makes no difference to the way the note is played.

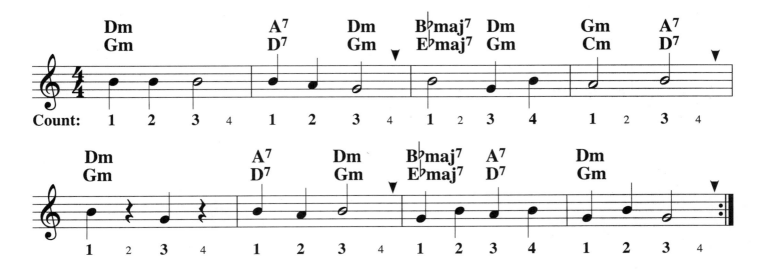

DUETS

A **duet** is a piece of music played by two instruments at the same time. This may be two saxophones, or a sax and a guitar, or a piano and a singer for example. The following example is a duet for two saxophones, using the note **B** along with the other notes you already know. The top line is for you to play and the bottom line is for your teacher. When you get to the end of bar four, remember to look at the top line of the second system of notation for your next bar rather than the bottom line of the first system (the teacher's part). Learn your part well so you don't get distracted by the other part. You can also practice your part along with the CD.

3.1

There are no breath marks in this piece, but there are several rests. You can breathe anywhere a rest occurs in the music. This is a good general rule to follow.

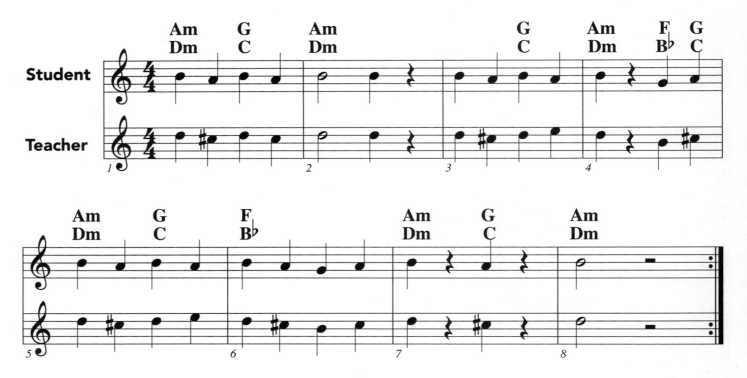

Here is another melody which makes use of the notes **G**, **A** and **B**. Once you can play a melody, try playing it from memory with your eyes closed. This will help you learn the fingerings of the notes and also make you more aware of your tone.

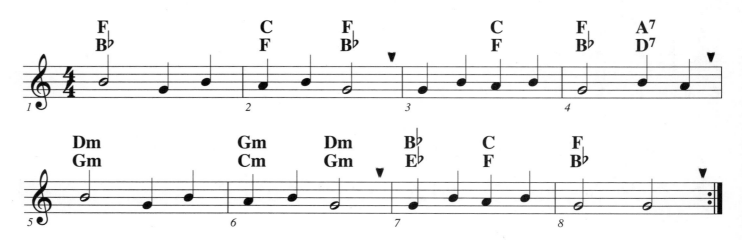

THE WHOLE NOTE AND WHOLE REST

This is a **whole note**. It lasts for **four** beats. There is **one** whole note in one bar of $\frac{4}{4}$ time.

Count: **1** 2 3 4

This symbol is called a **whole rest**. It indicates either **four** beats of silence or a **whole bar** of silence.

Count: 1 2 3 4

3.2

This duet features both the whole note and the whole rest. Remember to keep counting regardless of whether you see notes or rests in the music.

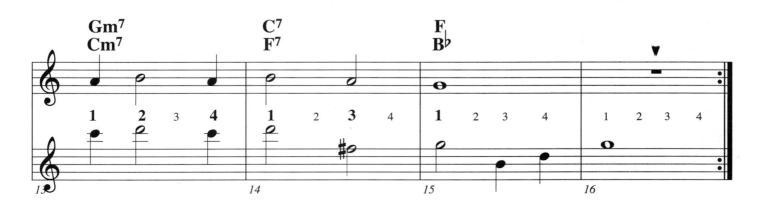

THE NOTE C

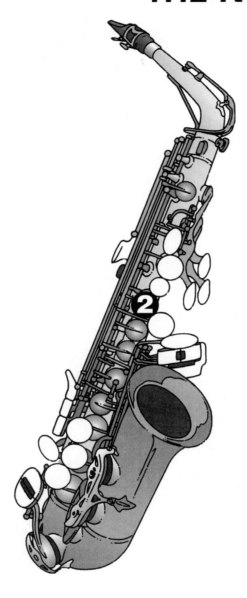

Notes written **above** the middle line of a staff usually have their stems going **down** on the left side of the note.

C Note

stem

This **C** note is placed in the **third** space of the staff.

Once you have memorized the fingering for the note **C**, play the following example which combines this new note with the other notes you have learnt.

 **3.3**

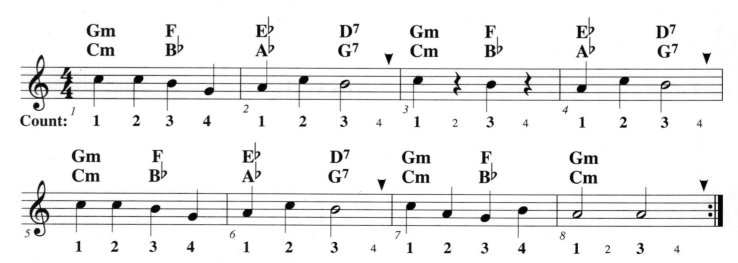

THE THREE FOUR TIME SIGNATUR...

3
4

This is the **three four** time signature.
It tells you there are **three** beats in each bar.
There are **three** quarter notes in one bar of $\frac{3}{4}$ tim...

3.4

THE DOTTED HALF NOTE

A **dot** written after a note extends its value by **half**.
A dot after a half note means that you hold it for **three** beats.
One dotted half note makes one bar of music in $\frac{3}{4}$ time.

Count: **1** 2 3

Here is a typical example of the way dotted half notes are used in $\frac{3}{4}$ time. As there are no rests in this example, breath marks are placed in every fourth bar after a dotted half note. From now on breath marks will only be placed every four bars to encourage you to develop more breath control. However, you can still breathe more often if you need to.

3.5

LESSON FOUR

THE NOTE F

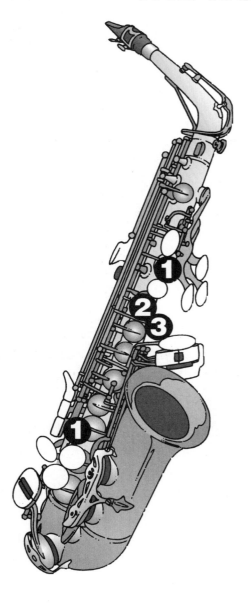

F Note

This **F** note is placed in the **first** space of the staff.

 4.0

This tune features the note **F**. It has an unusual sound. Play it slowly and smoothly. Notice the dotted half note in the final bar.

SLURS

A **slur** is a curved line above or below two or more different notes. It indicates that the notes must be played smoothly (called **legato**). To play legato, only tongue the **first** note of the group and keep blowing while you change your finger positions for the other notes.

 **4.1**

Remember to tongue only the first note of each group of notes connected by the slur.

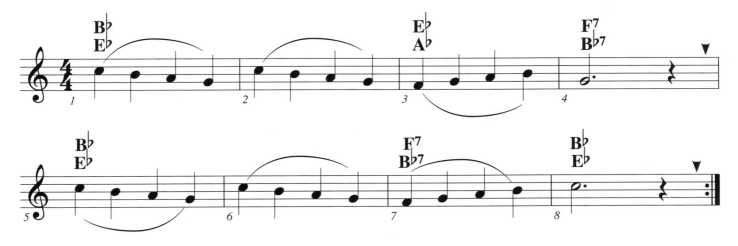

STACCATO

A dot above or below a note indicates that the note is to be played **staccato**, which means short and separate from other notes. This is the opposite of legato. To play a note staccato, make a short '**t**' action with your tongue, and cut off your breath as soon as you tongue the note.

 4.2

This example contains both staccato and slur marks. Note that the slur in bar 4 connects **two** notes rather than a group of notes.

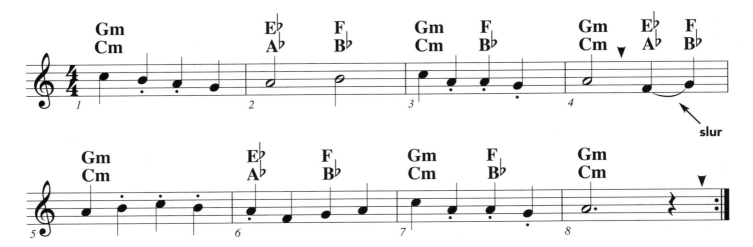

THE NOTE B FLAT (B♭)

 This is a **flat** sign.

When a flat sign is placed in front of a note, it **lowers** the note by an interval known as one **semitone** or one **half step**. Therefore the note **B♭** is one semitone **lower** than B. Since the difference in pitch between the notes A and B is one **whole tone** (two semitones or one **whole step**), **B♭** is also one semitone **higher** than **A**.

Other ways of playing **B♭** can be found in the index of fingerings on pages 210 to 213.

B♭ (B Flat) Note

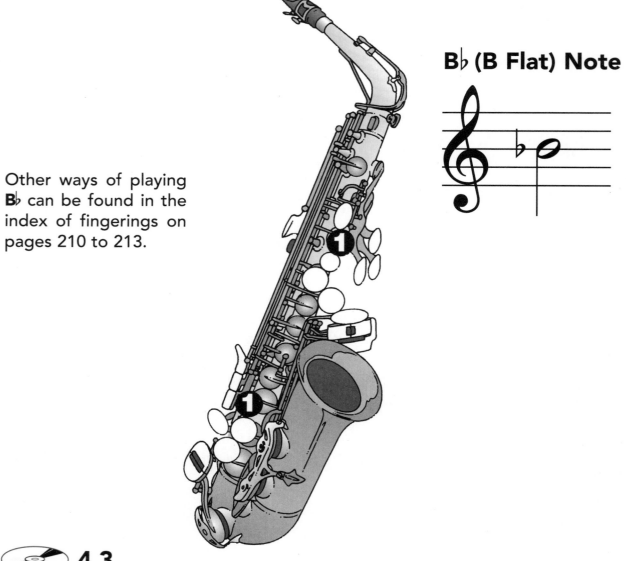

4.3

The flat sign affects **all** B notes within the bar in which it appears. Eg: in bars 1 and 4 the ♭ sign appears before the first B in each bar. The flat also applies to all other B notes within that particular bar. The effect of a flat sign is **cancelled by a bar line**, meaning that a **new** flat sign is needed to indicate a new **B♭** note in the following bar.

KEY SIGNATURES

Instead of writing a flat sign before every B♭ note, it is easier to write just one flat sign after the treble clef. This means that **all** B notes on the staff are played as B♭, even though there is no flat sign placed before the note. This is called a **Key Signature**. See page 45 for more information on key signatures.

4.4 Duet

This duet uses a key signature, which tells you to play all B notes as **B♭**. To play duets well, you need to be able to listen to yourself and the other player at the same time. Learn your part well and then try listening to both parts as you play.

4.5

Sometimes it takes only two or three notes to create a good saxophone part for a song. In a song like this, where and how the notes are played is the most important thing.

LESSON FIVE

THE LEAD-IN

Not all music begins on the first beat of a bar. In such cases, notes which come before the first full bar are called **lead-in notes** (or pick-up notes). When lead-in notes are used, the last bar is also incomplete. The notes in the lead-in and the notes in the last bar add up to one full bar.

 5.0   When the Saints go Marchin' in.

This early Jazz standard was a favorite with brass bands in New Orleans. It contains **three lead-in notes**. On the recording there are **five** drumbeats to introduce this song. This gives you a whole bar, plus one beat to get the feel of the tempo before the lead-in. Notice the **B♭** note written as a key signature in this song, reminding you to play all B notes as **B♭**. The teacher's part here is **swung**, as indicated by the symbol next to the title. Swing rhythms are common in Jazz and are discussed in detail in lesson 12.

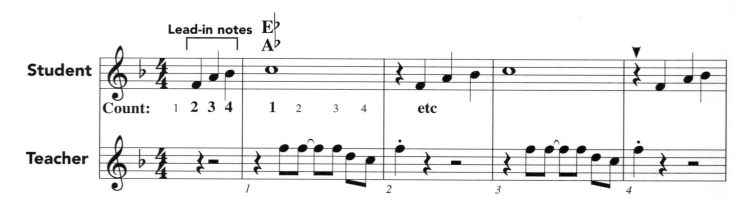

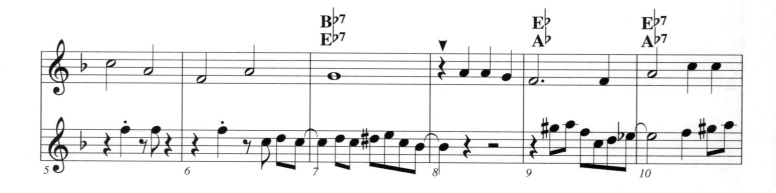

THE COMMON TIME SIGNATURE

C This symbol is the **common time** signature.
Common time is the same as $\frac{4}{4}$ time.

 5.1 **A Winter's Night**

P. Gelling

In this duet there is only **one** lead-in note.

THE TIE

A **tie** is a curved line written above or below two or more notes with the **same** position on the staff. When a tie appears, tongue the **first** note only, and to sustain it for the value of both notes. A tie may occur either **across a bar line**, or **within one bar**. The following example contains ties in bars 3, 5-6, 7-8, 11, 13-14, and 15-16.

5.2

12 BAR BLUES

The example below is a **12 bar Blues**, which is a progression of chords that repeats every 12 bars. 12 bar Blues are common in many styles of music including Blues, Jazz and Rock. All saxophone players need to know how to play a 12 bar Blues.

5.3

BREATHING TECHNIQUE

One of the most important elements of saxophone playing is a consistent and relaxed approach to breathing and breath control. A good sax player always produces a strong, even tone and sounds relaxed regardless of the difficulty of the music being played. Outlined below are some breathing exercises which will help you gain more control over the way you breathe when playing and give you a solid consistent approach which will eventually become automatic, enabling you to forget about breathing and concentrate totally on the music you are making.

A good way of developing your breathing technique is the use of visualisation. When you breathe **in**, think of an inflatable life raft which fills automatically when you pull out the plug. This will help you equate breathing in with relaxation. When you breathe **out**, think of a tube of toothpaste being slowly squeezed from the end (not the middle). This will help you use your breath economically in a controlled manner.

It is important to develop the habit of controlling your breathing from your diaphragm muscle (shown in the diagram below). As you breathe **in**, let the diaphragm relax downwards and allow the lungs to fill with air right to the bottom. Then breathe **out slowly**, squeezing gently from the diaphragm (like the tube of toothpaste) and see how long you can sustain your outgoing breath. The more control you have of your diaphragm, the easier you will find breathing when you play.

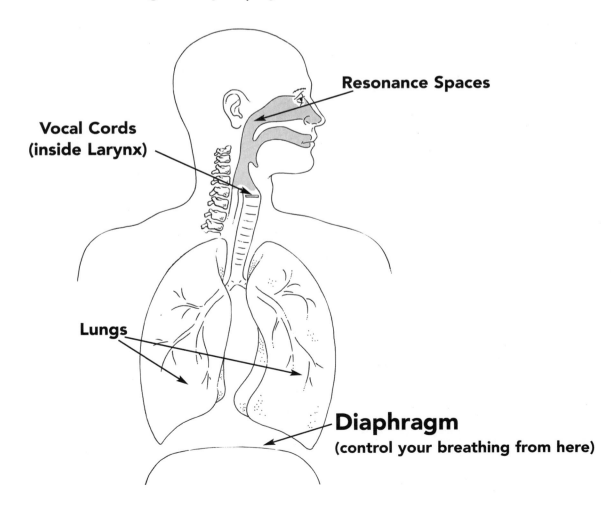

Resonance Spaces

**Vocal Cords
(inside Larynx)**

Lungs

Diaphragm
(control your breathing from here)

Breathing Exercise (Not on CD)

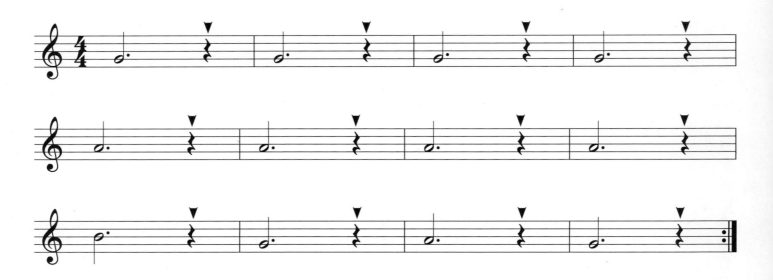

Breathing Exercise (Not on CD)

This example makes frequent use of whole notes. Practicing long notes is an excellent way of developing your tone as well as breath control. Aim for a **strong**, **even tone** throughout the example.

OTHER USEFUL EXERCISES

When playing wind instruments, it is common to use more air, movement and muscle activity than necessary. There are two common exercises which are useful for learning to use less force and less air when playing. The first of these is to slowly blow up a balloon, using slow sustained breaths controlled from the diaphragm. The idea is to take a comfortable breath using the technique described earlier and then breathe into the balloon using an even sustained amount of air pressure. Repeat this until the balloon is full.

The second exercise is to **sing** a melody in front of a lighted candle. This requires a more subtle release of air than blowing up a balloon, as the idea is to sing with as little effect on the flame of the candle as possible. Once you can sustain a note without moving the flame much, try beginning the note softly and gradually increasing the volume, then reverse the process. You could also try singing a whole verse from a song. As with all aspects of musicianship, be patient and you will see great improvement as long as you continue to practice.

POSTURE

The term "posture" refers to the way the body is held (e.g. straight, slumped, etc) and its position when sitting or standing. For playing wind instruments, it is best to stand rather than sit, as this allows the most open and unrestricted passage of air for both breathing and sustaining notes. If you are playing in a big band, you may have to sit. In this situation, it is essential to sit up straight but relaxed, as this will produce the best sound.

If you think of a situation where a sax player is performing with a band, it would look fairly dull if all the players stood straight in the one position all the time. Movement is a large part of any stage show. This means it is not always possible to maintain perfect posture. However, it is possible to keep the pathway from the diaphragm to the mouth open, flexible and relaxed most of the time, which means it is still possible to play and breathe comfortably while moving around. Relaxation and flexibility are keys to good posture regardless of standing or sitting position.

Incorrect

The spine is not straight and the head and pelvis both tilt forward. In this position, it is not possible to move freely or produce the best sound.

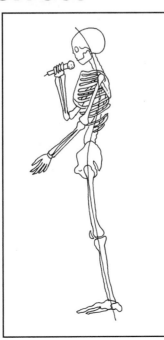

Correct

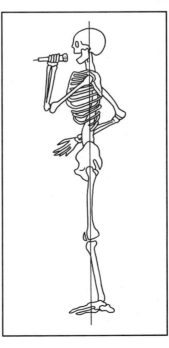

The spine is comfortably straight and in line with the head, legs and pelvis. This position keeps the airways open and makes movement easy and comfortable.

LESSON SIX

THE EIGHTH NOTE

💿 6.0   How to Count Eighth Notes

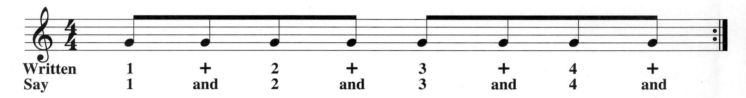

When you begin playing songs containing eighth notes, take them slowly at first until you gain control of all the notes. Once you are comfortable with the whole tune, gradually increase the tempo until you can play along with the CD. Since there are more notes now, you may need to breathe every two bars at first. You do not have to wait for a breath mark to breathe. Most sheet music does not contain breath marks so it is up to you to decide the best place to breathe. Notice the use of ties which occur on the last eighth note of each group in the following example. Remember to count to yourself as you play.

💿 6.1

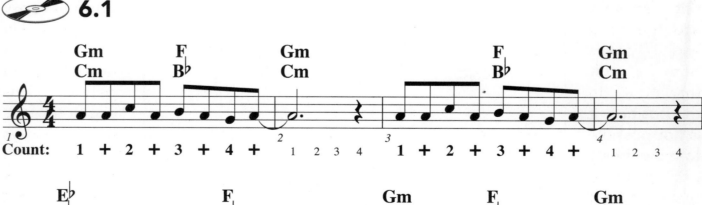

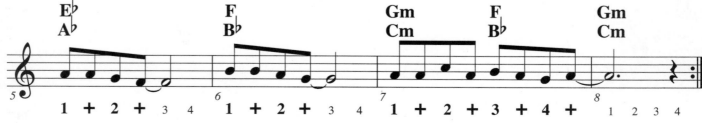

THE NOTE E

E Note

This **E** note is placed on the **first** line of the staff.

6.2   Desert Winds

P. Gelling

This example contains the note **E**. It also features slurs covering groups of notes.

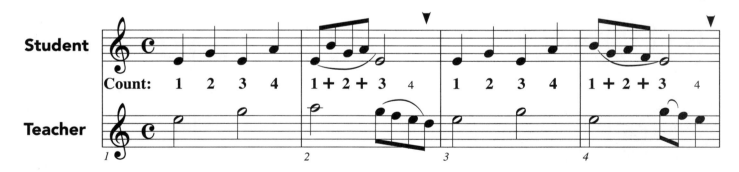

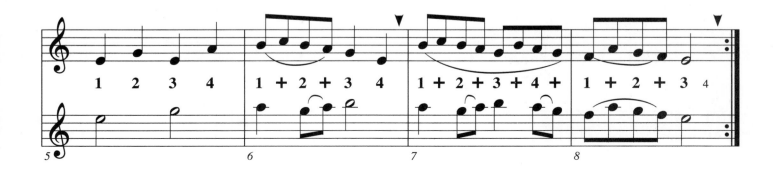

THE NOTE D

D Note

This **D** note is placed in the space **below** the staff.

6.3

This example is a minor key 12 bar Blues. It makes repeated use of the note **D**. Once again, take care with the timing of the tied notes.

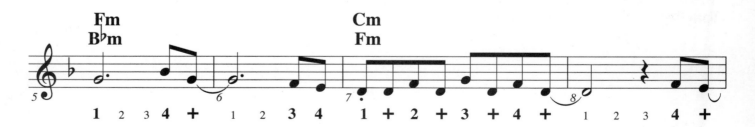

LESSON SEVEN

THE NOTE D IN THE MIDDLE REGISTER

D Note

Middle register D

one octave

Low register D

This new **D** note is **one octave higher** than the previous D note. An **octave** is the range of eight notes between a note and its next repeat higher or lower.

Octave key

LT ▶

D in the middle register uses the same fingering as **D** in the low register, but with the **octave key added**. The octave key is played by rolling the **left thumb** forward and up from the thumb rest. Practice this movement many times until it becomes automatic.

The Four Saxophone Registers

The range of notes on most instruments is divided into **registers**. The term "register" is used to describe a range of notes that have a similar tonal quality. This is something you will be able to hear more easily as your playing develops. The saxophone has **four** registers which are shown below.

The Low Register
B♭ to C♯

The Middle Register
D to C♯

The High Register
D to F♯

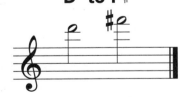

The Altissimo Register
Above F♯

USING THE OCTAVE KEY

Practice alternating between **D** in the low register and **D** in the middle register as shown below. All you need to do is move your thumb on and off the octave key.

The following example contains the note **D** in both the low and middle registers. When using the octave key, try to keep the tone as even as possible between registers.

7.0

Up to this point, all of the notes you have learnt have been in the **low register** of the saxophone except for the note **D** in the **middle register** which you have just learnt. This D note is exactly **one octave** above the low D. You can also use the octave key to create higher versions of all the other notes you have learnt. Eg: if you finger an **E** note and add the octave key, this produces an **E** in the **middle register** which is exactly **one octave** above the lower E. Once you are comfortable using the octave key to play the notes D and E in the middle register, try using the octave key with the note F, then G, then with all of the other notes you know. To play the higher version of each note, all you have to do is maintain the fingering and add the octave key. The examples on the following page use the notes **D, E, F, G** and **A** in the middle register along with other notes you already know. The following exercise alternates between notes in the low register and notes in the middle register. Take it slowly at first.

Alternating Between Low and Middle Registers

Middle register notes using the octave key

Here is a melody which uses the new notes you have just learnt. To become familiar with them, say the names of all the notes to yourself as you watch the written music.

RIFFS

The following example uses what is commonly known as a **riff**. A riff is a short musical idea (usually one, two or four bars long) which can be altered and varied to fit a chord progression. This one is an example of a riff applied to the 12 bar Blues progression.

7.1

LESSON EIGHT

THE NOTE F SHARP (F♯)

 This is a **sharp** sign.

A **sharp sign** is used to indicate that a note is played a semitone higher than its original pitch. In this case, the note **F♯** is one semitone **higher** than **F**. Like flat signs, a sharp sign is written immediately before the note to which it applies.

F♯ Note

 8.0

Here is an example which makes use of the note **F♯**.

THE NATURAL SIGN

 This is a **natural** sign.

A natural sign cancels the effect of a sharp or flat for the rest of that bar, or until another sharp or flat sign occurs within that bar. Notice the alternation between **F** natural (**F♮**) and **F♯** in example 8.1.

8.1

8.2

Now try this 12 bar Blues solo which makes use of **sharp**, **flat** and **natural** signs. It also uses the note **B♭ in the middle register**. The fingering is the same as the **B♭** you already know, but the **octave key** is added. There are no breath marks here, but the best place to breathe is at the end of each phrase – at the end of the tied notes.

THE DOTTED QUARTER NOTE

 A dot written after a quarter note indicates that the note is held for **one and a half beats**.

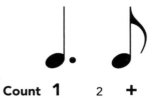 A dotted quarter note is often followed by an eighth note.

Count 1 2 +

 8.3

Count 1 2 + 3 4 1 2 3 4 + 1 2 + 3 4 + 1 2 + 3 4

This four bar melody is made up almost entirely of dotted quarter notes and eighth notes.

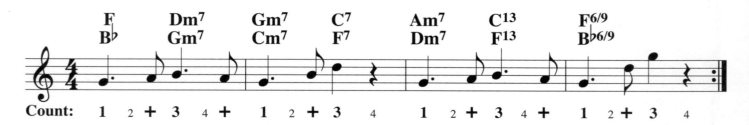

Count: 1 2 + 3 4 + 1 2 + 3 4 1 2 + 3 4 + 1 2 + 3 4

 **8.4**

The rhythm figure shown here is often used for horn section riffs.

LESSON NINE

THE NOTE LOW C

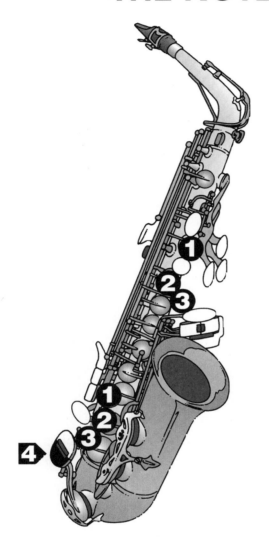

C Note

← leger line

Low C is placed just below the staff on a short line called a **leger line.**

Playing Low **C** requires the use of the fourth finger on the right hand as shown in the above diagram. Low notes can be difficult to control at first, so don't worry if you can't sustain the low C note at first. Like all other aspects of saxophone playing, it becomes easier with practice. The following example makes frequent use of the low **C** note.

9.0

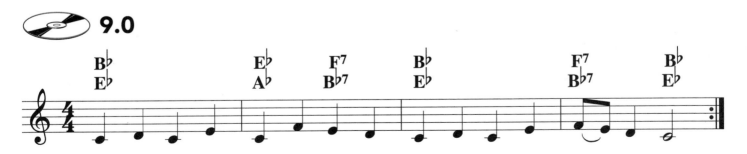

THE C MAJOR SCALE

A **major scale** is a group of eight notes that produces the familiar sound:

Do Re Mi Fa So La Ti Do

You now know all of the notes needed to play the **C major scale**.

C   D   E   F   G   A   B   C

The notation for the C major scale is shown below. The number underneath each note indicates its position in the scale. These numbers are called **scale degrees**. The distance from the first to the eighth note of a major scale is **one octave**. The names of the first and last notes of a major scale are always the same.

9.1   C Major Scale

KEY OF C MAJOR

When a song consists of notes from a particular scale, it is said to be written in the **key** which has the same name as that scale. For example, if a song contains notes from the **C major scale**, it is said to be in the **key of C major**. The following song is written in the key of C major.

9.2   Lavender's Blue

THE G MAJOR SCALE

The **G major scale** starts and ends on the note **G** and contains an **F#** note. Play the following G major scale and notice that it still has the familiar sound **Do Re Mi Fa So La Ti Do.** The F# note in this scale is played with the same fingering as the low F#, but with the octave key added. Notice once again the scale degrees written under the notes.

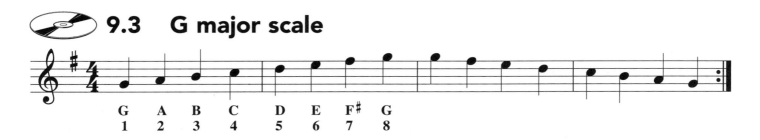

MORE ABOUT KEY SIGNATURES

On page 27 you were introduced to key signatures. A **key signature** consists of one or more **sharps or flats** written after the treble clef, or in the case of the key of C major **no** sharps or flats. Because the **G major scale** contains the note **F#**, the key signature for the **key of G major** will consist of an **F#** note written after the clef.

 This is the key signature for the key of **G major**. It has **one** sharp sign after the treble clef.

 The C major scale contains no sharps or flats, therefore the key of **C major** contains **no** sharps or flats.

Lavender's Blue in the Key of G Major

It is possible to play any melody in more than one key. On the previous page you learnt this song in the key of C major. Here is the same song in the key of **G major**. Changing the key of a piece of music is called **transposing**. This process will be discussed in detail in lesson 17.

THE KEY OF F MAJOR

The **F major scale** starts and ends on the note **F**, and it contains a **B♭** note instead of a B note. Play the F major scale below and listen for the **Do Re Mi Fa So La Ti Do** sound. Songs that use notes from the F major scale are in the **key of F major** and hence contain the note **B♭**. The key signature containing the note B♭ which was introduced on page 26 is the key signature of **F major**. Go back through the book and look for other examples of the key of F major.

F Major Scale

9.4   Folk Dance

P. Gelling

Here is a lively folk melody in the key of F major. You will need to breathe where the rest occurs at the end of bar 4. Make a habit of looking through tunes to find the best places to breathe before you begin playing.

LESSON TEN

SYNCOPATION

Here is another rhythm figure using dotted quarter notes. This time the eighth note is played first and the dotted quarter note is played off the beat. This creates an effect known as **syncopation**, which means displacing the normal flow of accents, usually from **on** the beat to **off** the beat. Practice this example slowly at first and count carefully as you play.

10.0

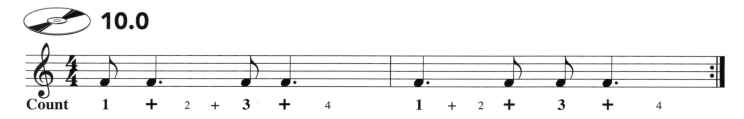

10.1 Swing Low Sweet Chariot

This well known spiritual makes frequent use of the syncopated rhythm shown above. If you have trouble with any of the timing in this song, practice the rhythm figures on one note at first as in example 10.0.

THE EIGHTH REST

 This is an **eighth rest**.
It indicates **half a beat of silence**.

The use of eighth rests on the beat is a very common way of achieving syncopated rhythms as shown in the following examples.

10.4

This one is a riff style 12 bar Blues. Play it slowly at first and take care with the timing.

Another common way of creating syncopated rhythms is the use of ties. Here is a rhythm similar to the one used in example 10.2. The difference is that it uses **ties** instead of rests on the beat.

10.5

10.6 Jamaica Farewell

This well known Caribbean song makes very effective use of syncopated rhythms using ties. It is written here in the key of F Major.

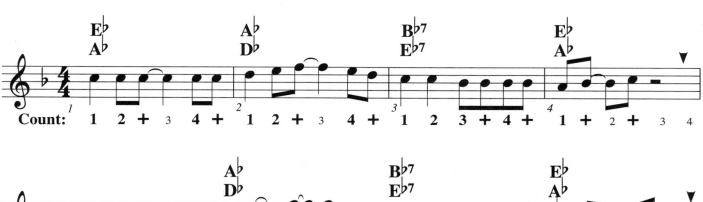

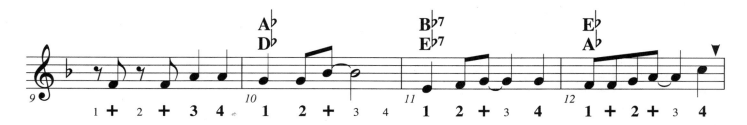

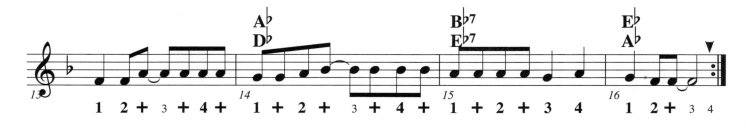

LESSON ELEVEN

THE NOTE E FLAT (E♭)

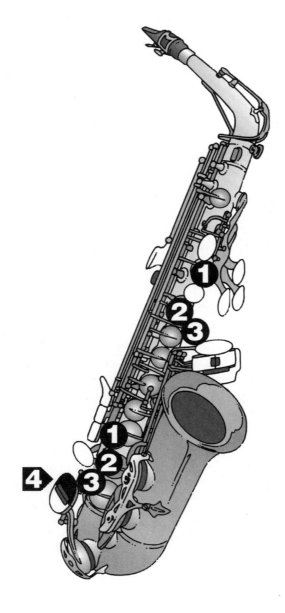

E♭ Note

11.0

This example makes extensive use of the note **E♭** with much alternation between E♭ and E♮. The third and fourth bars are played up an octave in the middle register. E♭ in the middle register uses the same fingering as the low register but with the octave key added.

THE BLUES SCALE

A common sound used for improvising in Blues, Rock and Jazz is the **Blues scale**. It sounds great when played on the saxophone. Written below is the C Blues scale.

 **11.1 C Blues scale**

 **11.2**

Here is an example of the type of musical line that can be created from the Blues scale.

ENHARMONIC NOTES

There is often more than one way of writing a particular note. Eg: the note **F sharp** can also be called **G flat**. These two notes have exactly the **same sound** and the **same fingering**. Therefore, either spelling of the note may occur in the written music. This is called **enharmonic** spelling of the same note. The **C Blues scale** is often written using a G♭ note instead of an **F♯** note. The following example uses both versions of this note.

11.3

Once you are comfortable playing the Blues scale in the low register, try playing it over two octaves. Use the octave key to play the **C** note in the middle register.

C Blues Scale Over two Octaves

11.4   Follow Me Home

P. Gelling

This 12 bar Blues solo makes use of the Blues scale in both the low and middle registers.

TWO OCTAVE C MAJOR SCALE

As well as the Blues scale, it is important to be able to play the major scale in more than one register. The following example shows the C major scale over two octaves. Try playing it with your eyes closed and say the names of the notes to yourself as you play.

C Major Scale Over two Octaves

 **11.5**

This example demonstrates a melody which uses the higher octave of the C major scale.

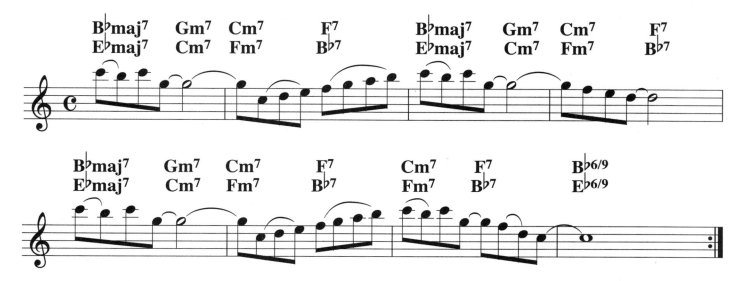

Here is an exercise to help you become more familiar with all the notes over two octaves.

MIXING DIFFERENT SCALES

It is worth comparing the notes of the Blues scale with those of the major scale. Here are the notes of both scales. The numbers written under the note names are the **scale degrees** which indicate the position of each note in the scale.

C Major Scale

C	D	E	F	G	A	B	C
1	2	3	4	5	6	7	8

C Blues Scale

C	E♭	F	G♭	G	B♭	C
1	♭3	4	♭5	5	♭7	8

Notice that the Blues scale contains both the ♭**5** and the ♮**5**. It does not contain the degrees **2** or **6**. Altogether, the Blues scale contains **six** different notes, whereas the major scale contains **seven** different notes. The major scale used by itself does not sound very bluesy. However, in Blues, Rock and Jazz, melodies often contain notes from both of these scales as shown in the following 12 bar Blues.

11.6   **Mixed Up Blues**

P. Gelling

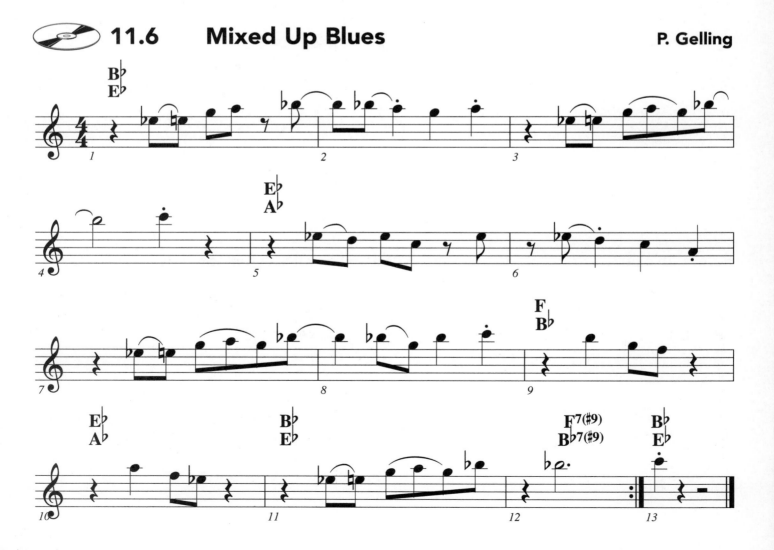

LESSON TWELVE

THE TRIPLET

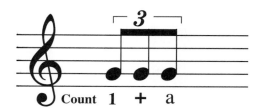

Count 1 + a

A **triplet** is a group of **three** evenly spaced notes played within one beat. Eighth note triplets are indicated by three eighth notes grouped together by a bracket (or a curved line) and the numeral **3**. The eighth note triplets are played with one third of a beat each. Triplets are easy to understand once you have heard them played. Listen to example 12 on the CD to hear the effect of triplets.

12.0

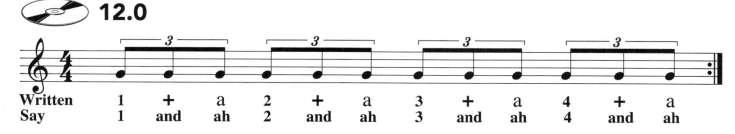

| Written | 1 | + | a | 2 | + | a | 3 | + | a | 4 | + | a |
| Say | 1 | and | ah | 2 | and | ah | 3 | and | ah | 4 | and | ah |

Triplets sound great when combined with the notes of the Blues scale as shown in the following example.

12.1

SWING RHYTHMS

Since the early 20th century there have been many new styles of music which use a rhythmic feeling called **swing**. These styles include Blues, Jazz, Gospel, Soul, Rock and Funk. A **swing rhythm** is created by tying together the first two notes of a triplet. There are several different ways of writing swing rhythms. To understand them it is worth using one musical example written in various ways. Example 12.2 has the first and second notes of each triplet tied together. Play this example and listen to the feeling created by the rhythm.

12.2

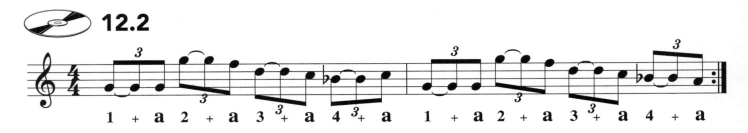

Instead of tying the first two notes of the triplet group, a quarter note can be used. The quarter note grouped with an eighth note by a triplet bracket shows clearly that the first note is worth two thirds of the beat, while the second note is worth only one third. Play the following example and notice that it sounds the same as the previous one. This is just a different way of writing the rhythm.

A third way to write the same rhythm is to notate the whole thing in eighth notes and to write the swing marking at the start of the music. Jazz players usually write swing rhythms in this manner, as it is easier to read. Shown below is the same example written in this manner.

FIRST AND SECOND ENDINGS

The following song contains **first and second endings**. The **first** time you play through the song, play the **first ending** ([1.___]), then go back to the beginning. The **second** time you play through the song, play the **second ending** ([2.___]) instead of the first. This one is a real challenge, so be patient with it. Learn your part well and then try playing along with the recording, as well as playing it with your teacher.

12.3 **Sidewalk Strut** P. Gelling

LESSON THIRTEEN

THE NOTE C SHARP (C#)

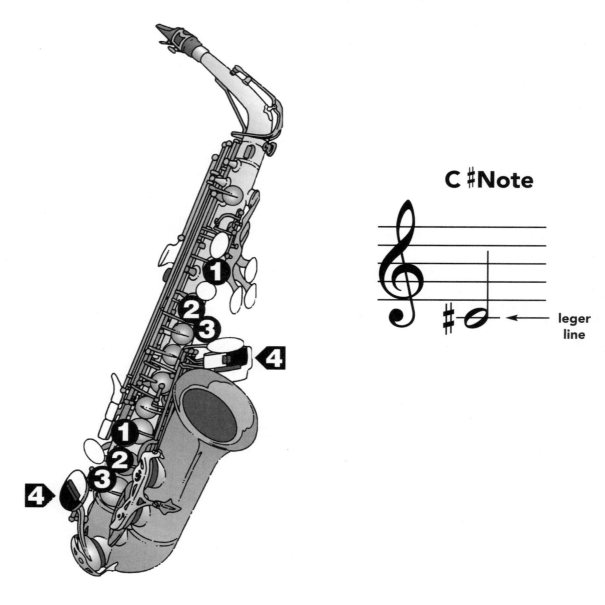

C # Note

leger line

 **13.0**

Here is an example using the note **C#**, along with other notes. Play it slowly and be sure to play all the correct sharps, flats and naturals.

A HIGHER C SHARP (C#) NOTE

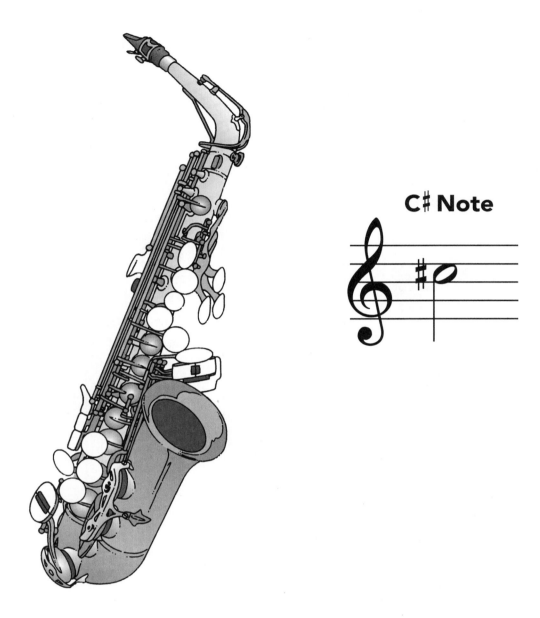

C# Note

THE D MAJOR SCALE

This **C#** note is easy to play, as it doesn't require the use of any fingers. You can also play **C#** an octave higher by adding the octave key. Once you know the note **C#**, you can play the **D major scale**, which is shown below. Notice the **key signature of D major** which consists of two sharps (**F#** and **C#**). Learn this scale well and then transpose some melodies from earlier in the book to the key of D major. Begin with simple melodies and gradually work up to more difficult ones.

THE NOTE HIGH D

High D Note

This **D** note is written above the second leger line above the staff.

Shown below is the **D** major scale over two octaves. The top note is the high D shown above. Both **C♯** notes use the same fingering and that you add the octave key for the higher one.

13.1 The Mountain Stream

P. Gelling

This piece is written in the key of **D major**. Once you can play it, try playing it in the lower octave and then transposing it to the keys of C, F and G.

THE NOTE D FLAT (D♭)

The note **D♭** is exactly the same as **C♯**. They are enharmonic notes. This means you already know three fingerings for a **D♭** note. Here is an example which shows these notes as both **C♯** and **D♭**. Name the notes to yourself as you play.

13.2

LESSON FOURTEEN

THE NOTE G SHARP OR A FLAT

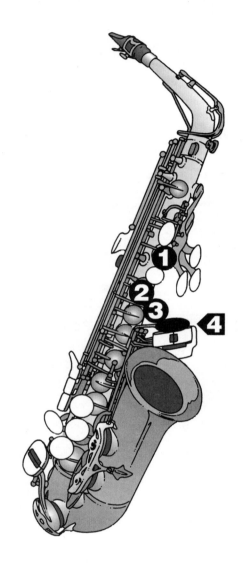

G# Note, A♭ Note

G# and **A♭** are enharmonic notes and therefore share the same fingering. As with other notes, you can also play the same note an octave higher by adding the octave key. Here is an example which features both octaves of the note written as both **G#** and **A♭**.

 **14.0**

THE A MAJOR SCALE

Written below is the A major scale. It contains three sharps - **F♯**, **C♯**, and **G♯**. Practice it until you have it in your memory and then play it with your eyes closed, visualizing the fingering for each note as you play.

14.1   Waltz Around

P. Gelling

Here is a **Jazz Waltz** in the key of **A major**. Try transposing it to the keys of **C**, **G**, **D** and **F**.

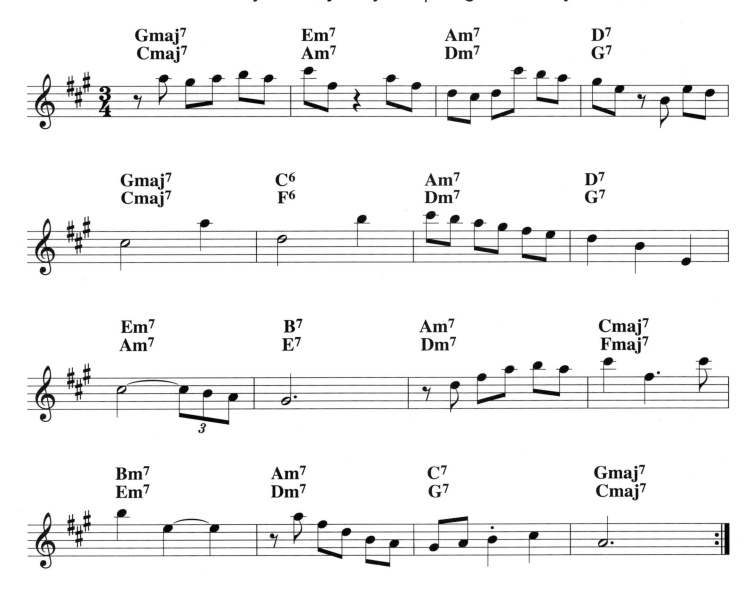

THE E MAJOR SCALE

The following example demonstrates the E major scale. It contains four sharps - **F#, C#, G#** and **D#**. As with previous new notes and scales, practice it until you have it in your memory and then play it with your eyes closed, visualizing the fingering for each note as you play.

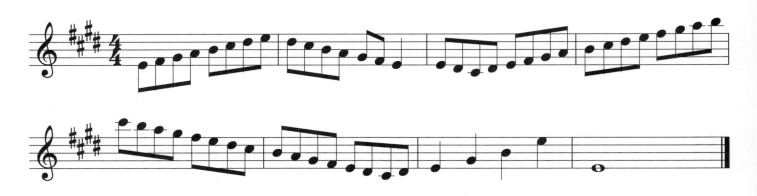

14.2   **Into the Sun**   **P. Gelling**

Here is a Pop melody in the key of **E major**. Once you have learned it, try transposing it to all the other keys you know.

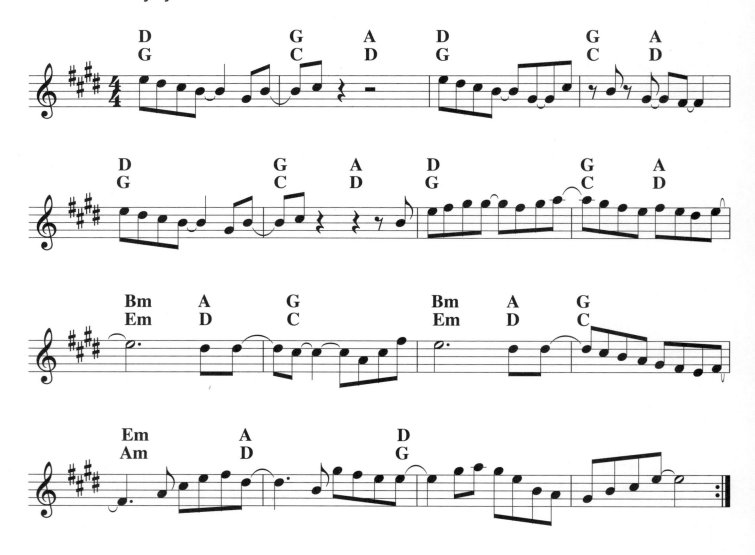

LESSON FIFTEEN

THE CHROMATIC SCALE

You now know all the different notes used in western music (twelve in all). This includes all the natural notes (**A B C D E F G**), plus **B♭**, as well as **F♯, C♯, G♯** and **D♯**. Because each sharp notes has another name as a flat, you also know **G♭, D♭, A♭** and **E♭**. **B♭** can also be called **A♯**, so when you add them all together, you have covered every possible note. If you play all twelve notes in succession, you get the **chromatic scale**, which contains all possible notes between a given note and its next repeat an octave higher or lower. All of the notes in a chromatic scale are **one semitone** apart. To get to know all possible ways of describing any note in a given key, it is a good idea to call notes all notes which are not natural to the key **sharps when ascending** and **flats when descending**.

The following example demonstrates two octaves of the **C chromatic scale**. Take it slowly at first and memorise all the fingerings so you can play it smoothly and easily without hesitation. It is a good idea to make the chromatic scale part of your daily practice, as a good knowledge of the chromatic scale makes it easy to quickly transpose any melody, as well as making it easier to learn any new scale.

C Chromatic Scale

Once you can play the C chromatic scale, you already know all other chromatic scales, e.g. to play the **E chromatic scale**, you simply start on the note **E** and play all possible notes until you arrive at the next E note one octave higher or lower, as demonstrated in the following example which contains two octaves of the E chromatic scale. You can find the fingerings for the top two notes (**D♯** and **E**) on page 85.

E Chromatic Scale

MORE ABOUT MAJOR SCALES

So far you have learned six different major scales - **F**, **G**, **C**, **D**, **A** and **E** major. The key of **C** contains no sharps or flats, while **G**, **D**, **A** and **E** all contain **sharps**. The key of **F** contains one **flat** (**B♭**). There are also other keys which contain flats. Once you know the pattern of tones and semitones which makes up a major scale, it is easy to create a major scale starting on any note. Written below are the notes of the **C** major scale with the pattern of tones and semitones written below the note names.

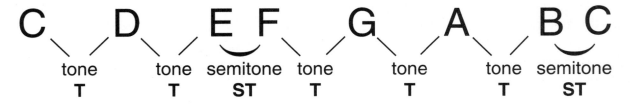

The distance between each note is a tone except for **EF** and **BC** where the distance is only a semitone. As mentioned earlier, once you know the pattern of tones and semitones used to create the C major scale, you can build a major scale on any of the twelve notes used in music. It is important to memorize this pattern, which is shown below.

Tone   Tone   Semitone   Tone   Tone   Tone   Semitone

The **semitones** are always found between the **3rd and 4th**, and **7th and 8th** degrees of the scale. All the other notes are a tone apart.

Shown below are the scales of **B♭**, **E♭** and **A♭** major which all contain flats. memorize each one and analyse them to determine how many flats there are in each one and which degrees these flats occur on.

LESSON SIXTEEN

PLAYING IN ALL KEYS

After you have learnt all the notes of the chromatic scale, it is a good idea to practice playing in every key. If you are playing with a singer, you will have to play songs in whatever key suits their particular voice. That could be **F♯** or **D♭** for example. Keyboard players tend to like the keys of **C**, **F** and **G**, while **E** and **A** are fairly common keys for guitar. Horn players like flat keys such as **F**, **B♭** and **E♭**. So you can see it is essential to learn to play equally well in every key.

A good way to learn to play in all keys is to use the **key cycle** (also called the cycle of 5ths or cycle of 4ths). It contains the names of all the keys and is fairly easy to memorise.

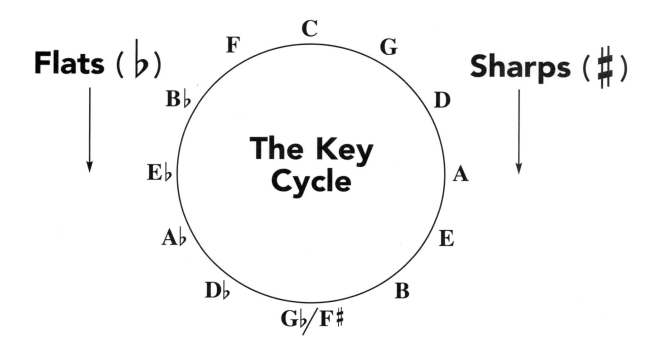

Think of the key cycle like a clock. Just as there are 12 points on the clock, there are also 12 keys. **C** is at the top and it contains no sharps or flats. Moving around clockwise you will find the next key is **G**, which contains one sharp (**F♯**). The next key is **D**, which contains two sharps (**F♯** and **C♯**). Progressing further through the sharp keys each key contains an extra sharp, with the new sharp being the 7th note of the new key, the other sharps being any which were contained in the previous key. Therefore the key of **A** would automatically contain **F♯** and **C♯** which were in the key of D, plus **G♯** which is the 7th note of the A major scale. As you progress around the cycle, each key introduces a new sharp. When you get to **F♯** (at 6 o'clock), the new sharp is called **E♯** which is enharmonically the same as **F**. Remember that **enharmonic** means two different ways of writing the same note. Another example of enharmonic spelling would be **F♯** and **G♭**. This means that **G♭** could become the name of the key of **F♯**. The key of **F♯** contains six sharps, while the key of **G♭** contains six flats.

If you start at **C** again at the top of the cycle and go anti-clockwise you will progress through the flat keys. The key of **F** contains one flat (**B♭**), which then becomes the name of the next key around the cycle. In flat keys, the new flat is always the 4th degree of the new key. Continuing around the cycle, the key of **B♭** contains two flats (**B♭** and **E♭**) and so on.

Written below are the key signatures for all the major scales that contain sharps.

	G Major	D Major	A Major	E Major	B Major	F# Major
Sharps	F#	F# C#	F# C# G#	F# C# G# D#	F# C# G# D# A#	F# C# G# D# A# E#

The sharp key signatures are summarised in the table below.

*The new sharp **key** is a fifth interval higher*

Key	Number of Sharps	Sharp Notes
G	1	F#
D	2	F#, C#
A	3	F#, C#, G#
E	4	F#, C#, G#, D#
B	5	F#, C#, G#, D#, A#,
F#	6	F#, C#, G#, D#, A#, E#

*The new sharp **note** is a fifth interval higher*

Written below are the key signatures for all the major scales that contain flats.

	F Major	B♭ Major	E♭ Major	A♭ Major	D♭ Major	G♭ Major
Flats	B♭	B♭E♭	B♭E♭A♭	B♭E♭A♭D♭	B♭E♭A♭D♭G♭	B♭E♭A♭D♭G♭C♭

The flat key signatures are summarised in the table below.

*The new flat **key** is a fourth interval higher*

Key	Number of Flats	Flat Notes
F	1	B♭
B♭	2	B♭, E♭
E♭	3	B♭, E♭, A♭
A♭	4	B♭, E♭, A♭, D♭
D♭	5	B♭, E♭, A♭, D♭, G♭,
G♭	6	B♭, E♭, A♭, D♭, G♭, C♭

*The new flat **note** is a fourth interval higher*

* Intervals are discussed in detail in lesson 21.

The following example demonstrates one octave of the major scale ascending and descending in every key. Learning scales may not seem as interesting as playing tunes, but a little effort at this stage will pay off very well later on. Memorise the fingering for each scale and then try playing it with your eyes closed while imagining how the notation for the scale would look. Once you have learnt all the scales, you will be able to play melodies confidently in any key and be able to improvise in any key much more easily.

Here are some exercises to help you get more comfortable playing in any particular key. Each of them is written in a different key, but they are intended to be played in all keys. The first one shows the use of third intervals in the key of E♭ major. You could also play a scale in fourths, fifths sixths or sevenths. **Intervals** are the subject of **lesson 21**.

This one alternates between the note B and every other note in the B major scale, both ascending and descending.

Don't forget to practice the chromatic scale in every key. Here it is in the key of G♭.

Finally, here is one which alternates between the note A and every other note in the A chromatic scale, once again ascending and descending. This one covers all possible intervals within an octave.

LESSON SEVENTEEN

TRANSPOSING

Transposing or transposition means changing the key of a piece of music. This can apply to a scale, a riff, a short melody, or an entire song. The ability to transpose is an essential skill for a sax player to develop. The easiest way to transpose is to write the **scale degrees** under the original melody and then work out which notes correspond to those scale degrees in the key you want to transpose to. Here is an example of a melody transposed from the key of **F** to the key of **G**. Try this same technique with other tunes from earlier in the book, or any other tunes you know.

Melody in F Major

Same Melody in G Major

USING THE KEY CYCLE

A good way to become more confident playing in all keys is to take a phrase and play it in every key in order of sharps and flats around the key cycle as shown in the following example which moves around the cycle anticlockwise (adding a new flat for each new key and then continuing through the sharp keys). It is also important to repeat the process going clockwise around the cycle. Write the scale degrees under the notes at first if necessary, and sing them to yourself as you play. If you hope to play Jazz, this ability is essential, as the majority of Jazz tunes modulate around the key cycle in this manner. Make this process part of your everyday practice. The eventual aim is to be able to pick up your horn and be able to play any melody in any key instantly.

ACCIDENTALS

In the previous examples, the melody consists entirely of notes from the major scale. However, many melodies use notes from outside the major scale, particularly in styles such as Rock, Funk, Blues and Jazz. These "outside notes" are called **accidentals**. An accidental is a temporary alteration to a note or notes from a particular key. These accidentals often come from the chromatic scale starting on the same note as the major scale of the key the music is written in. Therefore, if you have a piece of music in the key of C which contains notes which are not in the C major scale, you can relate these notes to the **C chromatic scale**.

C Chromatic Scale

C C#/Db D D#/Eb EF F#/Gb G G#/Ab A A#/Bb BC

PRACTICAL USE OF ENHARMONIC NOTES

The "in between" notes in the chromatic scale can be described as either sharps or flats. Because of the way scales and chords are constructed, flats are used more often than sharps. Here once again is the C chromatic scale with scale degrees written under the notes. The scale degrees written here relate to the natural notes and the flat notes. The sharps are **enharmonic equivalents**, which means they are the same pitch (e.g C# =Db and F# =Gb).

C C#/Db D D#/Eb E F F#/Gb G G#/Ab A A#/Bb B C

1 b2 2 b3 3 4 b5 5 b6 6 b7 7 1

The following example demonstrates a melody in the key of C which contains notes from outside the C major scale. The extra notes can all be found in the chromatic scale.

15.0 Key of C

1 1 7 b7 6 5 b3 3 5 6 5 b7 6 5

#4 5 b5 4 3 b3 3 4 #4 5 b7 7 1

The following examples are the same melody transposed to the keys of F and G. Once again, you should transpose this melody to all the other keys in the key cycle. It is worth learning to play the chromatic scale starting on any note of the key cycle. If you do this, it will be easier to play melodies in any key and also make it easier to transpose any melody that you learn in any key.

Same Melody in F

Same Melody in G

Here is another melody in the key of G. Analyze its degrees and then transpose it to all twelve keys.

LESSON EIGHTEEN

MORE ON BLUES SCALES

Like the major scale, it is important to be comfortable with the Blues scale in every key. The following example demonstrates the Blues scale moving **up chromatically** through all the keys. Once again, memorise the fingerings until you can play the whole example smoothly and evenly without looking at the notation. Then try reversing the order of the keys (moving down chromatically).

Blues Scales in all Keys

Once you are comfortable with the scales themselves, try inventing a short riff from the Blues scale in one key and then playing the riff in all keys as shown in the following example. If you have trouble with this, memorise all the scale degrees of the riff before transposing it. The riff shown here begins on the flattened 7th degree of the key.

Blues Scale Phrase in all Keys

To finish this lesson, here are two solos derived from Blues scales in different keys. The first one is a driving Rock solo derived from the **A** Blues scale.

15.1 Drivin' Home

P. Gelling

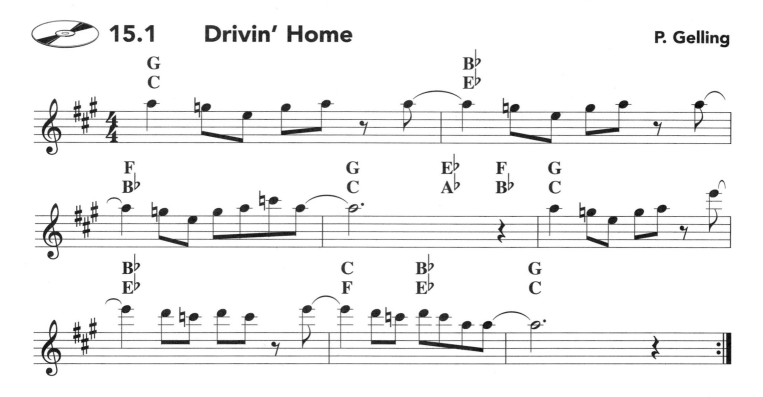

15.2 Blues After Midnight

P. Gelling

This one is a Blues in the key of **F♯** which is enharmonically the same as **G♭**. Once you can play these solos, try transposing them to other keys.

LESSON NINETEEN

IMPROVISATION

One of the most exciting aspects of saxophone playing is **improvisation**. Improvisation means creating your own melodies as you play. Learning to improvise well takes some time, but once you know how to play in any key and have reasonable control of eighth note rhythms, you have all the tools you need to start developing your improvising ability. A good way to work on improvisation is to use a **repetition and variation** approach, as shown in the following examples. The first one shows a simple lick created from the G Blues scale. The term **"lick"** means a short phrase. Jazz, Blues and Rock players usually learn and create new licks every day to constantly expand their improvisation skills.

16.0

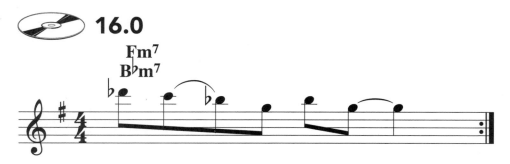

The easiest way to develop an idea is to repeat it and vary it slightly on each repetition. In example 16.1, the basic lick is extended out into a four bar phrase by using this approach. On the recording the band repeats the example without the saxophone, leaving space for you to play the phrase or improvise your own.

16.1

Another way to develop an idea is to use a **call and response** or question and answer approach. This time the basic idea is answered by a different idea before the first idea is repeated. This approach works well when you are playing with a vocalist or another instrumentalist. Once again the recording leaves space for you to play on the repeat.

16.2

One more way of developing a basic idea is to keep the same rhythm but vary the pitches. This approach works well when moving between different chords, as demonstrated in the following example.

16.3

The following solo uses elements of all the approaches demonstrated in this lesson. Make a habit of taking a basic musical idea and developing it in various ways. This way your improvisation will develop continuously until eventually you can do it without even thinking about it.

16.4 **Falling Down Blues**

P. Gelling

DEVELOPING RHYTHMIC CONTROL

To become a good musician, it is essential to have control over exactly where in the bar you play and where you don't play. A good way to develop this ability is to concentrate totally on rhythm by using only one note and to play it in all different rhythmic positions within a bar. The following examples begin with a pair of eighth notes played on each beat of the bar and then move on to groups of four notes played in various different positions. Take care with the final one which is more syncopated. It is important to count as you play the following examples and try to memorize each one.

IMPROVISING WITH SET RHYTHMS

The next step is to play these short rhythm figures between different pitches to create riffs, and eventually to improvise with the rhythms. The idea is that you can play any pitches you like, but the rhythm remains the same every bar. The following example uses the final rhythm from the previous page played on various pitches derived from the F Blues scale.

17.0

Here are some more set rhythm examples which use eighth note rhythms covering two bars. In these examples, the rhythm is shown first on one note and then as a riff using various pitches.

To finish this section, here is a solo which contains almost everything you have learnt so far. Practice it slowly to begin with and then try to play along with the recording. You should now make a habit of **improvising** on a melody once you have learnt it (but make sure you can play it correctly first). Try varying the notes and timing of some of the songs and examples in the book, and then make up some of your own phrases based on them. The 12 bar Blues is an excellent progression for improvising, particularly with the Blues scale. As you progress through the rest of the book, you will learn more about scales, chords, rhythms and expressive techniques which will help you improve your improvising. As well as this, you should do as much playing by ear over chord progressions as possible. Make improvisation a part of your daily practice routine. It is also essential to play with other musicians regularly, experiment and have fun!

18. Roll and Tumble Blues

P. Gelling

Section 2

LESSON TWENTY

NEW NOTES

So far you have learnt all the notes between **middle C** and **high D**. In this lesson, you will learn two new low notes (**B** and **B♭**), which complete the notes in the low register, and four new high notes above high D which complete the high register. Any notes above high **F♯** are in the altissimo register and will be dealt with later in the book. shown below are the fingerings for **B** and **B♭** in the low register. Remember that **B♭** is enharmonically the same as **A♯** .

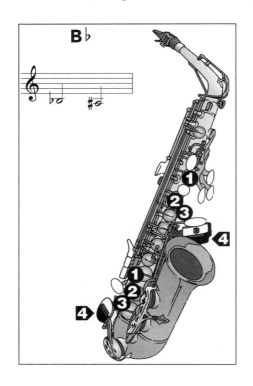

💿 19.0

Here is an example which makes use of both new notes. These very low notes may take some time to control properly, but stick with it, practice them for a short time each day and your perseverance will definitely pay off.

HIGH NOTES

Shown below are four new high notes above high D which complete the high register. Learn the fingerings from memory and then practice the following example which uses them. The high **F♯** or **G♭** note cannot be played on some saxophones. If this is the case with your horn, just play the second line of the example below.

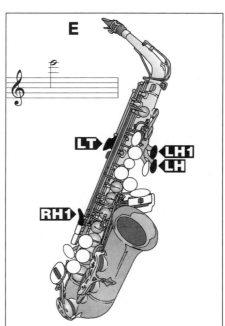

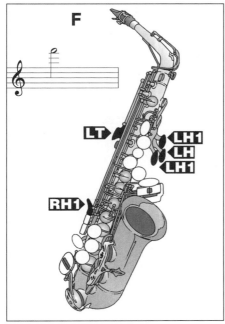

 **19.1**

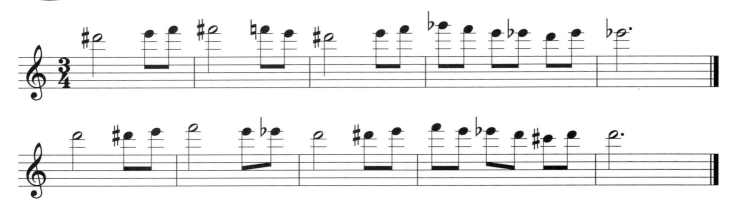

Once you have control of these new notes, Try playing a chromatic scale starting on low **B♭** and ending on high **F♯** as shown below. If you can't play the high F♯ on your particular instrument, end the ascending scale with the high **F**.

TWO OCTAVE SCALES

You now know enough notes to be able to play over two octaves in any key. It is important to practice all your scales (e.g. major scale, blues scale and chromatic scale) over two octaves ascending and descending. Try working on a different key each day. Practice scales and sequences over a range of two octaves in a particular key as well as transposing melodies to that key, and also improvising and inventing licks in the key. Next day, choose a new key and repeat the process. If you practice this way for a few months, you will notice a dramatic improvement in your playing and your musical knowledge.

THE 8va SYMBOL

The following example has the symbol **8va** above the music. This means it is played an octave higher than written. This symbol is often used for very high notes, as it makes them easier to read. When the notation returns to its normal pitch, the word **loco** is written above the music.

19.2

LESSON TWENTY ONE

INTERVALS

An interval is the distance between two musical notes. Intervals are measured in numbers, and are calculated by counting the number of letter names (**A B C D E F G A**) between and including the notes being measured. Within an octave, intervals are: **Unison** (two notes of the same pitch played or sung together or consecutively), **2nd**, **3rd**, **4th**, **5th**, **6th**, **7th** and **Octave** (two notes an octave apart). Thus **A** to **B** is a **2nd** interval, as is B to C, C to D etc. **A** to **C** is a **3rd** interval, **A** to **D** is a **4th**, **A** to **E** is a **5th**, **A** to **F** is a **6th**, **A** to **G** is a **7th** and **A** to the next **A** is an **octave**.

Intervals may be **melodic** (two notes played consecutively) or **harmonic** (two notes played at the same time). Hence two people singing at the same time are said to be singing in harmony.

INTERVAL QUALITIES

Different intervals have different qualities, as shown below:

Quality	Can be applied to
Perfect	Unisons, 4ths, 5ths and Octaves
Major	2nds, 3rds, 6ths and 7ths
Minor	2nds, 3rds, 6ths and 7ths
Augmented	All intervals
Diminished	All intervals

These intervals can be best explained with the aid of a chromatic scale. If you look at the one below, it is easy to see that since intervals are measured in semitones, they may begin or end on a sharp or flat rather than a natural note.

A A#/Bb B C C#/Db D D#/Eb E F F#/Gb G G#/Ab A

Perfect intervals are **4ths**, **5ths** and **octaves**. If you **widen** a perfect interval by a semitone it becomes **augmented** (added to). E.g. if you add a semitone to the perfect 4th interval **C** to **F**, it becomes the **augmented 4th interval C** to **F#**. Notice that the letter name remains the same–it is not referred to as C to Gb.

If you narrow a perfect interval by a semitone they become **diminished** (lessened). E.g. if you lessen the perfect 5th interval **D** to **A** by a semitone, it becomes the **diminished 5th interval D** to **Ab**. Again, the letter name remains the same–it is not referred to as D to G#.

Major intervals (2nds, 3rds, 6ths and 7ths) become minor if narrowed by a semitone and **minor** intervals become major if widened by a semitone. A **diminished** interval can be created by narrowing a perfect or minor interval by a semitone. An **augmented** interval can be created by widening a perfect or major interval by a semitone.

INTERVAL DISTANCES

In summary, here is a list of the distances of all common intervals up to an octave measured in semitones. Each new interval is one semitone wider apart than the previous one. Notice that the interval of an octave is exactly twelve semitones. This is because there are twelve different notes in the chromatic scale. Notice also that the interval which has a distance of six semitones can be called either an augmented 4th or a diminished 5th. This interval is also often called a **tritone** (6 semitones = 3 tones).

Minor 2nd - One semitone

Major 2nd - Two semitones

Minor 3rd - Three semitones

Major 3rd - Four semitones

Perfect 4th - Five semitones

Augmented 4th or Diminished 5th - Six semitones

Perfect 5th - Seven semitones

Minor 6th - Eight semitones

Major 6th - Nine semitones

Minor 7th - Ten semitones

Major 7th - Eleven semitones

Perfect Octave - Twelve semitones

Shown below is the notation all of the common intervals ascending within one octave starting and ending on the note C. Practice them for a short time each day and try to memorize the sound of each interval.

The next example demonstrates all of the common intervals descending within one octave starting and ending on the note B♭. These examples are only a starting point. If you want to become a good musician, it is important to learn all possible intervals up and down from **all twelve notes** of the chromatic scale.

INTERVALS IN SEQUENCES

Once you have a basic understanding of how intervals work, it is a good idea to practice playing scales in interval sequences. The following examples demonstrate intervals played through various major scales. Because of the pattern of tones and semitones within the major scale, you will find that various types of intervals occur rather than all being the one type. E.g. the exercise below shows the C major scale played ascending and descending in 2nds. All of the intervals are 2nds but some of them are major 2nds (e.g. C to D and D to E) and some are minor 2nds (e.g. E to F and B to C).

Following on from 2nds within a major scale, here is the F major scale played in 3rds. Once again, some are major and some are minor.

This example shows the A major scale played in 4ths. All of the intervals here are perfect 4ths except for D to G♯ which is an augmented 4th.

Here is the B♭ major scale played in 5ths. All of the intervals are perfect 5ths except for A to E♭ which is a diminished 5th.

This one demonstrates the G major scale played in 6ths. Again, some are major and some are minor. As the intervals get larger, these examples will probably become more difficult to play. Take them slowly at first but stick with it, as a good knowledge of intervals is essential for all musicians, especially players of transposing instruments such as the saxophone.

To finish off the intervals within an octave, this example shows the A major scale played in 7ths. As with previous interval studies you will find that some of the 7ths here are major and some are minor.

LEARNING INTERVALS IN ALL KEYS

In this lesson each interval pattern has been given in one key only, but it is important to practice each of these sequences in all keys to ensure you have a thorough knowledge of intervals. Depending on the key, you may not be able to get all of the notes, as some will be too low or too high depending on the register. Play each key in the most practical range and gradually expand the sequences to cover the entire range of the saxophone. Interval studies are the kind of thing that is important to practice every day, but only for a short time (e.g. 5 to 10 minutes per day). The better your knowledge of intervals is, the easier you will find it to transpose music. You will find it a lot easier to play the notes you hear in your mind when you are improvising if you have practiced all the intervals well, because **all melodies are a series of intervals**.

IDENTIFYING INTERVALS BY EAR

Since all melodies are made up of a series of intervals, it is essential to learn to identify intervals by ear and be able to reproduce them at will both with your voice and on your instrument. If you can sing something accurately, it means you are hearing it accurately. Here are some ways of developing your ability to identify and reproduce intervals. The example given in the first two exercises is a minor 3rd, but it is essential to go through these processes with **all** intervals.

1. Choose an interval you wish to work on (e.g. minor 3rds). Play a starting note (e.g. C) and sing it. Then sing a minor 3rd up from that note (Eb). Hold the note in your mind while you test its accuracy on your instrument. Then choose another starting note and repeat the process. Keep doing this until you are accurate every time. The next step is to sing the interval (in this case a minor 3rd) downwards from your starting note. Again, do this repeatedly until you are accurate every time.

2. Sing the same interval consecutively upwards and then downwards several times. E.g. start on C and sing a minor 3rd up from it (Eb). Then sing a minor 3rd up from Eb (Gb). Then another minor third up from Gb (Bbb - which is enharmonically the same as A). Then up another minor 3rd (C an octave higher than the starting note). Once you can do this, reverse the process (Start on C and sing a minor 3rd down to A, then another minor 3rd down and then another, etc).

3. Play and sing a starting note (e.g. C) and then think of it as the first degree of the chromatic scale - sing "one". Now sing the flattened second degree of the scale - sing "flat two". This note is a minor 2nd up from your C note (a Db note). Then sing the C again ("one"). Then sing the second degree of the scale (a D note - sing "two"). Next, sing your C Note again ("one"). Continue in this manner all the way up the chromatic scale until you reach C an octave above. The entire sequence goes: 1, b2, 1, 2, 1, b3, 1, 3, 1, 4, 1, b5, 1, 5, 1, b6, 1, 6, 1, b7, 1, 7, 1, 8, 1. As with the previous exercises, once you can do this accurately (check your pitches on your instrument), reverse the process and sing downwards from the top of the scale, working your way down the chromatic scale again. The downward sequence goes 1(8), 7, 1, b7, 1, 6, 1, b6, 1, 5, 1,b 5, 1, 4, 1, 3, 1, b3, 1, 2, 1, b2, 1, 1, 1(8).

HARMONIC INTERVALS

As well as hearing intervals melodically (one note at a time), it is important to be able to hear them harmonically (two notes played together). Even though you cannot play harmonic intervals on the saxophone, it is essential to be able to recognise them because they will be played by the keyboard player or guitarist in any group and you will need to know how to respond to what they are playing. A good way to develop this ability is to have a friend play random harmonic intervals on either guitar or keyboard while you identify them. Keep your back to the instrument while you do this, so that you cannot identify the intervals by sight.

Shown below are some harmonic intervals. Write the correct name below each interval.

For more practice with intervals, write and play the correct note to form each of the indicated intervals above each note shown here. Write the intervals harmonically for practice, but you will have to play them as melodic intervals.

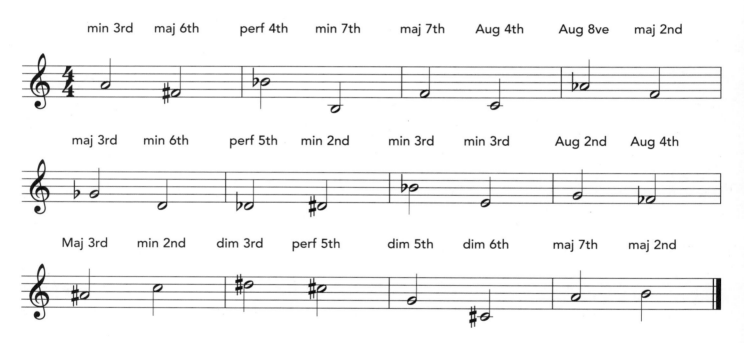

It is important to work at these things regularly until they become easy. Don't get frustrated if you can't hear intervals accurately at first. Most people have trouble with this. If you work at it for several months, you will see a dramatic improvement in your musical hearing, and will be able to improvise much more freely as well as being able to work out parts off CDs more easily.

THE SAXOPHONE AS A TRANSPOSING INSTRUMENT

There are **three basic tunings** for musical instruments, these being "**concert**" **or C instruments** (e.g. piano, guitar, flute or violin), **B flat instruments** (e.g. tenor sax, clarinet or trumpet) and **E flat instruments** (e.g. alto or baritone sax). What this means in practical terms is that if you play the same written note on each of these three types of instruments, a different note will sound for each of the three types. The reason for the different tunings is the actual length of the tubing required to make the instruments themselves, along with ease of playing. The **B♭** and **E♭** instruments are referred to as **transposing instruments**. If you play a C note on a B♭ instrument, the sound that actually comes out is a concert B♭ note. If you play a C note on an E♭ instrument, the sound that actually comes out is a concert E♭ note. Once you have a good knowledge of intervals, it is easy to understand the relationship between the three tunings. If you see a note written for a concert instrument (e.g C) you would have to play a note **one tone higher** on a B♭ instrument to get a concert C note to sound (play a D note). To sound a concert C note on an E♭ instrument, you would need to play a note a **major sixth higher** (an A note). This is a general transposing principle with these instruments whenever you are playing with other musicians or are reading a part written for a concert instrument. Most sheet music is written for concert instruments, so transposing is an essential skill for any horn player to develop. If you are called in at short notice to play with a band, you will often be expected to transpose your part to the correct key immediately. If you can't do this, they are likely to call another horn player who can!

Shown below is a C major scale written for concert pitch instruments, along with the correct transpositions for B♭ instruments (up a tone - key of D) and E♭ instruments (up a major 6th - key of A). As a result of these transpositions, all the notes come out sounding in the same key (concert key of C).

TRANSPOSING CHART

Shown below are the necessary transpositions for **Concert**, **B♭** and **E♭** instruments to play together in the same key. The more familiar you are with intervals, the easier you will find both transposing melodies and quickly finding the correct key to play with other instruments. Work on intervals for a short time each day until you are thoroughly familiar with them in all keys.

C or "Concert Instruments" Guitar Piano Flute Violin	B♭ Instruments Tenor Sax Soprano Sax Clarinet Trumpet	E♭ Instruments Alto Sax Baritone Sax
C	D	A
C♯ or D♭	D♯ or E♭	B♭ or A♯
D	E	B
E♭ or D♯	F	C
E	F♯ or G♭	C♯ or D♭
F	G	D
F♯ or G♭	G♯ or A♭	D♯ or E♭
G	A	E
G♯ or A♭	B♭ or A♯	F
A	B	F♯ or G♭
B♭ or A♯	C	G
B	C♯ or D♭	G♯ or A♭

LESSON TWENTY TWO

UNDERSTANDING CHORDS

A **chord** is a group of 3 or more notes played simultaneously. Different types of chords can be formed by using different combinations of notes. The most basic type of chord contains three different notes and is called a **triad**. The most common triad is the **major chord**. All major chords contain three notes taken from the major scale of the same letter name. These three notes are the 1 (first), 3 (third) and 5 (fifth) degrees of the major scale, so the **chord formula** for the major chord is:

Chord Symbol

| C |

1   3   5

The C Major Chord

Notes in Chord

C	E	G
1	3	5

The C major chord is constructed from the C major scale. Using the above chord formula on the C major scale below, it can be seen that the C major chord contains the notes **C**, **E** and **G**.

 C Major Scale

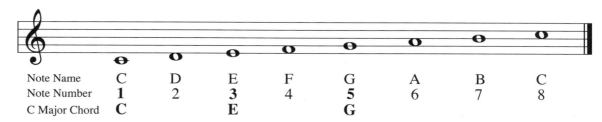

Note Name	C	D	E	F	G	A	B	C
Note Number	1	2	3	4	5	6	7	8
C Major Chord	C		E		G			

Once you have the correct notes for a C chord they can be arranged in any order. As long as the notes are still C, E and G, you still have a C chord. E.g. a C chord could be played C E G, or E G C, or G C E, or even G E C. These various arrangements of the notes within a chord are called **inversions**.

Chords can be played more easily on some instruments than others. Two of the most common instruments used for chord playing are the guitar and the keyboard. It is possible to double (or even triple) the notes of a chord on these instruments. It is not possible to play chords on the saxophone, but they can be played as arpeggios. It is worth learning all inversions of each arpeggio, as this enables you to identify all the degrees of the chord (called chord tones) more easily, which means you can respond quickly to what is being played by other musicians you are playing with regardless of the harmony. If you know the notes and inversions of chords well, it also makes it a lot easier to play in a horn section where a chord is made up of individual notes played by different instruments. It is also recommended that you learn at least a bit of basic keyboard so you get used to hearing the sound of all of the notes of chords together instead of one at a time. Most of the great horn players also have an excellent knowledge of keyboard harmony.

ARPEGGIOS

Up to this point, everything you have learnt has been based on the use of scales. There are also other important groupings of notes called **arpeggios**. An arpeggio is a chord played one note at a time. The value of arpeggios is that they enable you to play lines which fit chord progressions perfectly, since every note of an arpeggio is a note of the accompanying chord. Written below is a **C major arpeggio** which consists of the notes **C, E** and **G**. These are the **root**, **third** and **fifth** of a **C major chord**.

Here is an **F major arpeggio** which consists of the notes **F, A** and **C**. These are the root, third and fifth of an **F major chord**.

Like scales, it is important to be able to play arpeggios in every key. The following example demonstrates major arpeggios played around the key cycle.

This example shows another important method of practicing arpeggios - ascending and descending through all inversions of the chord. As you learn each new type of chord, practice all arpeggios in this manner. Don't forget to learn each type of arpeggio on all 12 notes of the chromatic scale.

Once you know the notes contained in a chord, it becomes much easier to improvise over that chord. Chord changes usually occur on the first beat of a bar and also on the third beat of the bar in $\frac{4}{4}$ time. If you play a note of the chord on these beats, your melody will always fit well with the chord being played by the other musicians. There are no real wrong notes in music and you can actually play any note against any chord, but when you sustain a note it becomes more important that the note relates directly to the chord unless you are deliberately trying to create dissonance or unless the progression quickly moves to another chord. The following melody demonstrates the use of chord tones using the triads of **C**, **F** and **G** major.

20.

LESSON TWENTY THREE

CHORD CONSTRUCTION

Chords are usually made up of combinations of major and minor third intervals. As mentioned previously, the simplest chords are made up of three notes and are called **triads**. There are **four** basic types of triads: **major**, **minor**, **augmented** and **diminished**. Examples of each of these are shown below along with the formula for each one.

C Major Chord

Chord Symbol

| C |

Notes in Chord

C	E	G
1	3	5

Minor Third — **5 G**

Major Third — **3 E**

1 C

C Minor Chord

Chord Symbol

| Cm |

Notes in Chord

C	E♭	G
1	♭3	5

Major Third — **5 G**

Minor Third — **♭3 E♭**

1 C

C Augmented Chord

Chord Symbol

| C+ |

Notes in Chord

C	E	G♯
1	3	♯5

Major Third — **♯5 G♯**

Major Third — **3 E**

1 C

C Diminished Chord

Chord Symbol

| Cdim or C° |

Notes in Chord

C	E♭	G♭
1	♭3	♭5

Minor Third — **♭5 G♭**

Minor Third — **♭3 E♭**

Minor Third — **1 C**

Using the formulas on the previous page, you can easily work out the notes for any type of triad beginning on any note. E.g, to form an **A major** chord you would begin with the note **A** and then add a **major 3rd** above it (**C#**) and then a **minor 3rd** above that (**E**). To form a **D# diminished** chord, you would begin with a **D#** note and then add a **minor 3rd** above it (**F#**) and then another minor 3rd above that (**A**). To help you become more familiar with the four types of triads, write the required notes above the root notes shown below to create the triads indicated.

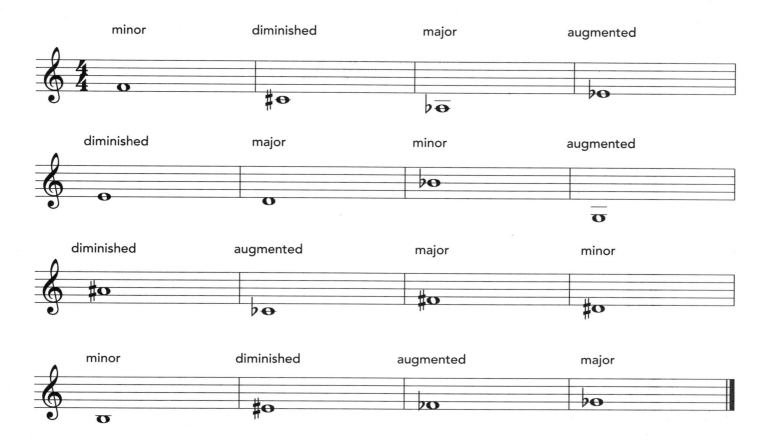

DOUBLE SHARPS AND DOUBLE FLATS

Sometimes in music, particularly when notating chords it is necessary to use double sharps (indicated by ✗) and double flats (indicated by ♭♭). The reason for this is the spelling of the intervals. E.g. a **B augmented** triad would contain the notes **B**, **D#** and **F ✗** . You will notice **F double sharp** is the same as **G natural**. The reason F double sharp is used is that the interval of a major 3rd above **D#** must contain the letter **F** and not the letter **G**; The same principle applies with double flats. E.g. an **E♭ diminished** triad would contain the notes **E♭**, **G♭** and **B♭♭** . The **B double flat** would be used instead of **A natural** because the minor 3rd interval above **G♭** must contain the letter **B** and not **A**. These are more examples of **enharmonic** notes. You may also have noticed the use of notes such as **C♭**, **F♭**, **B#** and **E#** in some of the previous examples. Although they are not common, these notes are used in music and are therefore worth learning.

For every type of chord there is a corresponding arpeggio. This means there are major, minor, augmented, diminished, dominant seventh and minor seventh arpeggios among others. The most common arpeggios used in Rock are major, minor and seventh arpeggios, so these are the ones which will be discussed in this book. Shown below is a **C minor arpeggio** which consists of the notes **C**, **E♭** and **G** which are the **root**, **flattened third** and **fifth** of a **C minor chord**.

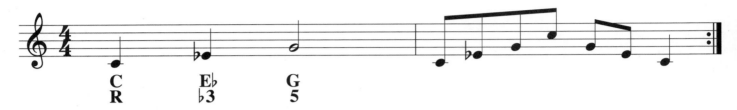

This is a **G minor arpeggio** which consists of the notes **G**, **B♭** and **D**. These are the root, third and fifth of a **G minor chord**.

Here are all the minor arpeggios between C minor and B minor played chromatically upwards. Try playing them downwards chromatically as well.

The riff played in the following 12 bar Blues consists entirely of notes from minor arpeggios. The chord symbols written above the music tell you which arpeggio you are playing in any given bar.

21.

CHORDS TRANSPOSED FOR ACCOMPANIMENT

The chord symbols above the above example relate directly to the arpeggios played by the saxophone. However, because the saxophone is a transposing instrument, these chord symbols will be in a different key to the one used by concert pitch instruments like piano or guitar. The following example shows the same riff with the accompanying chords for both the alto and tenor versions written above them. Because the riff is played in the key of C minor on the saxophone, the accompanying chords for the alto version are written in the key of E♭ minor while the chords for the tenor version are written in the key of B♭ minor. If you are still unsure about the relationship between the key you are playing in and the key the accompaniment is in, refer to the chart on page 101.

IMPROVISING WITH ARPEGGIOS

Once you are comfortable playing through a chord progression using arpeggios, try improvising more freely with the notes instead of simply running up and down the arpeggios (although this **is** an essential first step). If you have trouble, use some set rhythms until it becomes easier. The following example uses the same 12 bar Blues progression in **C minor**, but the lines are much freer both melodically and rhythmically. Notice that when a chord change occurs the line moves to the nearest note of the arpeggio of the new chord rather than starting on the root note of each new chord. This results in a much smoother and more logical melodic line.

AUGMENTED AND DIMINISHED ARPEGGIOS

Augmented and diminished chords are not as common as major or minor chords, but it is still important to learn them, as they do occur in many pieces of music as a way of creating tension before resolving to either a major or minor chord. Here are some examples demonstrating these chords. Listen to the CD to hear what they sound like. Don't forget to practice them in all keys.

C Augmented

C Diminished

Here is a progression which makes use of arpeggios of all four types of triads – **major**, **minor**, **augmented** and **diminished**.

LESSON TWENTY FOUR

SEVENTH ARPEGGIOS

One of the most important sounds in Rock, Funk, Blues and Jazz is the **dominant seventh chord**, usually just called the **7th chord**. 7th chords consist of four notes which are the first (1), third (3), fifth (5) and flattened seventh (♭7) notes of the major scale, so the **chord formula** for the seventh chord is:

<h1 style="text-align:center">1　3　5　♭7</h1>

A flattened seventh (♭7) is created by lowering the seventh note of the major scale by one semitone. This is the same ♭7 note that is found in the Blues scale. Notice that the seventh chord is simply a major chord with a flattened seventh note added. The example below demonstrates a **C7** arpeggio. Its notes are **C** (root), **E** (3rd), **G** (5th) and **B♭** (flattened 7th).

By using the formula **1 3 5 ♭7**, it is possible to build a dominant 7th chord or arpeggio on any note of the chromatic scale. Here is a **D7** arpeggio which consists of the notes **D** (root), **F♯** (3rd), **A** (5th) and **C** (♭7th).

Like everything else you have learnt, it is important to be able to play 7th arpeggios in all keys. In the following example, the arpeggios are played downwards; i.e. **R, ♭7, 5, 3, R**.

Here is a typical R&B sax riff which is made up entirely of notes from the arpeggios of the chords D7, G7 and A7. These are chords built on the **first**, **fourth** and **fifth** notes in the key of D. Chords built on these notes are known as chords $\bar{1}$, $\overline{IV}$ and $\overline{V}$, which are the most common chords used in Blues and R&B songs as well as many 1950's and 60's Rock and Roll songs.

23.0   **Slapback**   P. Gelling

ALTERNATING THIRDS

Another important sound commonly used in Rock and all its related styles is the use of both the minor and major third of a chord. There are literally thousands of sax, guitar and keyboard riffs which either alternate between the two thirds or begin on the minor third and then move to the major third. Here is an example of this sound in the **key of A**. The minor (or flattened) 3rd is **C** and the major 3rd is **C♯**. The notes of this solo come from a combination of the Blues scale (which contains the minor 3rd) and the A7 arpeggio (which contains the major 3rd).

23.1 Walkin' the Floor   P. Gelling

Here is a **12 bar Blues** solo in the key of **B♭** which makes use of many different intervals. Go through it and analyze the intervals and also the scale degrees against a **B♭ chromatic scale**. Notice the use of both major and minor 3rd degrees, as well as the flattened 5th and 7th degrees of the scale. The ♭**3**, ♭**5** and ♭**7** are known as **blue notes** and are particularly common in Blues.

24 Blue Note Blues

P. Gelling

LESSON TWENTY FIVE

RHYTHMS USING TRIPLETS

In lesson 19 you learnt the various placings of eighth notes both within a beat and within a bar. With triplets, there are three possible places within each beat that either a note or a rest may occur. When playing swing rhythms, the notes occur on the first and third parts of the triplet. The following examples demonstrate some other important rhythm figures derived from triplets. All of these rhythms are common in any song that swings, so it is essential to be familiar with them. Remember to count as you play the following examples and try to memorize each one.

Once you have memorized the above rhythms, Try using them to play your scales and arpeggios. This next example demonstrates the F Blues scale played with the second rhythm shown above.

Here is an A7 arpeggio played with the same rhythm.

As with eighth note rhythms, the next step is to play these short rhythm figures between different pitches to create riffs, and eventually to improvise with them. The following examples demonstrate riffs and lines created from combinations of the rhythms from this lesson and the previous lesson. Try making up some of your own set rhythms and begin improvising on different pitches. Experiment!

25.0

25.1

25.2

25.3

LESSON TWENTY SIX

EXPRESSIVE TECHNIQUES

As well as the notes and rhythms you play, there are several important expressive techniques which can add a lot of drama and excitement to your playing. One of the most common expressive techniques is the use of **grace notes**. Grace notes have no real time of their own. Rather, they are heard as an expression added to the note they are leading to. A grace note is indicated by a very small note with a stroke through its stem. This note is played immediately before the following note, which is held for its full value. listen to example 26 on the CD to hear the effect of grace notes.

26.0

The Following solo demonstrates some typical uses of grace notes. If you have trouble playing it at first, isolate the particular part you have difficulty with and practice it slowly and deliberately until you are confident, then try playing it at a faster tempo. As you will hear, grace notes can add a lot of expression to your sax playing.

26.1   **Shoe Shine Shuffle**

P. Gelling

VIBRATO

Another important expressive technique which is used in all styles of music is **vibrato**. Vibrato is a method of altering the quality of a note once it has been sounded. It is usually heard as a slight wavering of the pitch and volume of a note. Vibrato may be fast, slow or anywhere in between. The speed and width of vibrato are a matter of personal taste and often depend on the musical situation. There are several methods of producing vibrato on the saxophone. These involve movement of the diaphragm, the larynx, the jaw, the tongue and the lips either alone or in combinations. The easiest way to begin playing vibrato is to imagine you are a singer and to vibrate the larynx in a similar method to a singing vibrato. It is a good idea to exaggerate the vibrato at first and then ease off when you have control of it. Another method is to vibrate both the diaphragm and the larynx in a similar movement to laughing. Yet another method is to move the jaw up and down while you are holding a note. Vibrato is a very personal thing and may take some time to develop. It is probably a good idea to work with a teacher when you are learning vibrato, as it can be difficult to obtain a good vibrato sound at first. However, once you have some control of it, vibrato can add a lot of character and warmth to your playing. Another important aspect of learning is **listening**. You can learn a lot about vibrato by simply listening to players you admire and imitating their sound. By this stage in your playing, you should be listening to albums featuring sax playing every day. Listen to example 27 on the CD to hear the effect of vibrato.

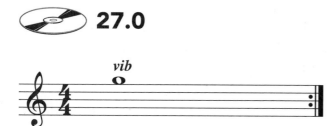

27.0

A good way to begin adding vibrato to your playing is to alternate between a note which has vibrato added to it and one that does not, as demonstrated in the following example.

27.1

Another good exercise is to begin a note without vibrato and then gradually add some vibrato to it.

27.2

The next stage is to play a riff and add vibrato to some of the notes. In general, it is more common to use vibrato on long notes, particularly at the end of a phrase.

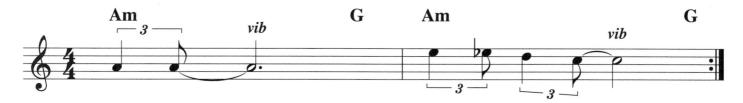

GROWLING

Another exciting sound commonly used by Blues and Rock sax players is **growling**. This effect is achieved by actually **singing** as you play the notes. The vibrations in your throat translate through the saxophone as a growling sound. Listen to the following example on the CD to hear the effect this produces. When the example repeats, try it yourself.

28.1   **Kelly's Blues**   P. Gelling

Here is a solo which makes use of the growling technique. Notice also the use of vibrato on some of the longer notes in this solo.

Here is a solo which uses grace notes, vibrato and growling. If you've come this far, you are definitely ready to play in a band and should begin jamming with other musicians if you're not already doing so. Another thing you should begin doing is transcribing sax solos from albums. You may wish to write the notes down or you may wish to learn them by ear, but transcribing is an important skill for any musician to develop. Make transcribing part of your daily practice routine. Listen for expressive techniques as well as just the notes and rhythms, and try to imitate what you hear as closely as possible.

29.   Swing That Thing

P. Gelling

LESSON TWENTY SEVEN

SIXTEENTH NOTES

This is a **sixteenth note**.
It lasts for **one quarter** of a beat.
There are **four** sixteenth notes in one beat.
There are **16** sixteenth notes in one bar of 𝄴 time.

Two sixteenth notes joined together.

Four sixteenth notes joined together.

Count: **1 e + a**
Say: one 'ee' and 'ah'

 ### 30.0 How to Count Sixteenth Notes

Count out loud as you play this example and remember to keep all the notes even in length and volume. Tap your foot on each beat and be careful not to tap in between the beats.

Count: 1   e   +   a   2   e   +   a   3   e   +   a   4   e   +   a

 ### 30.1

Here is a Funk riff which makes use of sixteenth notes.

As with other beat subdivisions (e.g. eighth notes and triplets) it is important to be able to play all your scales and arpeggios using 16th notes. Here are some examples. The first one is the F Blues scale over two octaves.

This one shows the arpeggios of D major and D minor played in 16th notes.

TEMPO MARKINGS

The term **tempo** refers to the **speed** at which music is played. As with dynamic markings, tempo markings come from Italian words. Some of them are listed below, along with their English translations. It is important to be able to recognize these markings and to be able to play comfortably at each tempo.

adagio (slowly)   *andante* (an easy walking pace)   *moderato* (a moderate speed)

allegro (fast)   *presto* (very fast)

TEMPO CHANGES

There are specific markings for changes in tempo. The most common ones are listed below.

accelerando (gradually becoming faster)

rallentando
or   (gradually becoming slower)
ritardando

ritenuto (*rit*) (immediately slower)   *a tempo* (return to the original tempo)

SIXTEENTH NOTE FIGURES

Sixteenth notes are commonly used within a beat in conjunction with eighth notes. The following examples demonstrate the Blues scales of F and F# using common rhythmic figures. It is a good idea to practice all your scales and arpeggios using these rhythms.

30.2

This riff makes use of both of the above rhythm figures.

Here are four more important 16th note figures. Practice each one on one note as shown below and then use them to play arpeggios and scales. When you are confident with each rhythm, try improvising with it.

Count   1   e   +   **a**   2   e   +   **a**   3   e   +   **a**   4   e   +   **a**

Count   1   **e**   +   **a**   2   **e**   +   **a**   3   **e**   +   **a**   4   **e**   +   **a**

Count   1   **e**   **+**   **a**   2   **e**   **+**   **a**   3   **e**   **+**   **a**   4   **e**   **+**   **a**

Count   1   **e**   **+**   **a**   2   **e**   **+**   **a**   3   **e**   **+**   **a**   4   **e**   **+**   **a**

LESSON TWENTY EIGHT

16TH NOTE SET RHYTHMS

A great way to work new rhythms into your playing is to write down short rhythmic phrases on one note which use the figure(s) you are learning. Then memorise the rhythm by singing it and then playing it and finally improvising with the rhythm. When you improvise with it you can choose any notes you like, but you must stick strictly to the set rhythm. This is only an exercise but the discipline it provides will greatly benefit your playing. The following examples demonstrate a set rhythm on one note and then a phrase using the set rhythm.

31.0

31.1

The next stage is to add ties or extra rests to the rhythm figures. Notice that the rhythm is exactly the same in both bars of this example. Practice the rhythm on one note at first if necessary. Set rhythms are very common in riffs played behind a vocalist and also in horn section parts. This means that the ability to memorize a rhythm quickly and then use it on different sets of pitches is an important skill for all horn players to develop.

31.2

REPETITION AND VARIATION

The following solo is based on several of the rhythms you have been learning. There is much repetition of rhythms in this solo. Repetition is important because it helps a listener to keep track and make sense of what you are playing. It also helps the other musicians you are playing with to follow you and complement what you are playing. Many of the best horn parts ever played are based on the elements of repetition and variation. The 16th notes in this solo are swung. Try swinging the 16th notes in other examples you have learned.

32.   Hangin' on the Corner

P. Gelling

LESSON TWENTY NINE

ARTICULATIONS

There are many different ways in which a note can be played, e.g. loud, soft, staccato, legato, etc. These different ways of playing a note are called **articulations**. The way you articulate notes can make a dramatic difference to the way the music sounds. There are specific markings which can be used in written music to indicate the articulation desired by the composer. Two examples of this are shown below. A short horizontal line directly above or below a note indicates that the note is to be held for its full written duration. This articulation is called **tenuto**. Another common articulation which you may already know is **staccato**, which means the note is to be played short and separate from other notes. Staccato is indicated by a dot placed directly above or below a note.

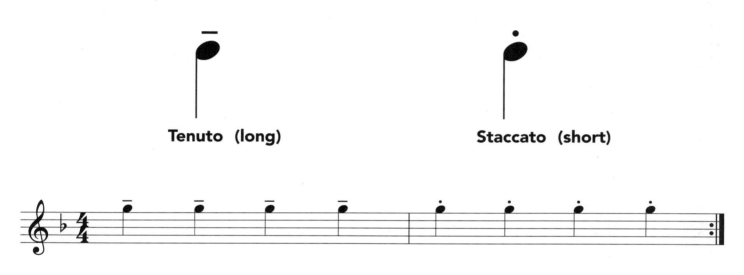

Tenuto (long) Staccato (short)

Most sheet music doesn't contain detailed articulation markings. Sometimes staccato notes are marked, but tenuto usually isn't. It is often assumed that most notes will be played tenuto (held for their written duration) The following example shows a G major scale alternating between tenuto (not indicated) and staccato. This is often described as long-short. Practice all your scales and arpeggios in this manner until it becomes natural to you.

Next, try reversing the articulations so that the staccato notes fall on each beat and the tenuto notes are off the beat. This is often described as short-long articulation. It is shown here using the A Blues scale.

The following riffs make use of both tenuto and staccato markings. Listen to the CD to hear the effect produced by the different articulations. Experiment with these articulations in your playing by applying them to phrases you already know well and then try improvising with them. The other important thing to do is to listen to albums featuring your favorite sax players and pay careful attention to how they articulate notes in different styles and situations. If you do this for even a few minutes each day, it won't take long before you begin to instinctively know how to articulate notes as you come to them.

 **33.0**

 **33.1**

Notice the use of swung 16th notes once again in this example.

ACCENTS

Another important aspect of articulating notes is the use of **Accents**. Accent markings are used to indicate notes which are to be played louder than other notes. There are two common types of accents, these being a tenuto accent (long) and a staccato accent (short). The long accent is indicated by a horizontal wedge mark above or below the note. The short accent is indicated by a vertical wedge mark above or below the note.

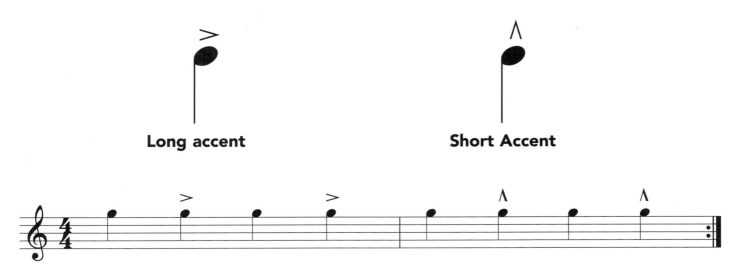

Long accent   **Short Accent**

As with all new articulations, it is a good idea to practice accents with scales and arpeggios. This example demonstrates both types of accents applied to the B♭ major scale

Here are some sax parts which make use of both types of accents. Try adding accents to phrases you already know and then try using accents in your improvising.

34.0

These next two examples use tenuto and staccato markings as well as accents.

34.1

34.2

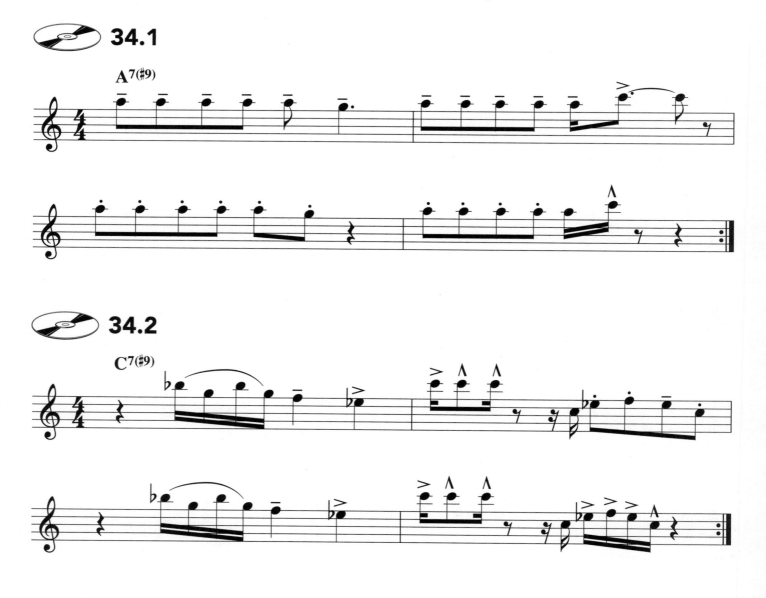

LESSON THIRTY

GHOST NOTES

A **ghost note** is the opposite of an accent. It is a note played softer than other notes. A ghost note is indicated by brackets placed either side of the note as shown below. The amount of "ghosting" is up to the individual player. A ghost note can be anything from about half the volume of unghosted notes right down to barely audible.

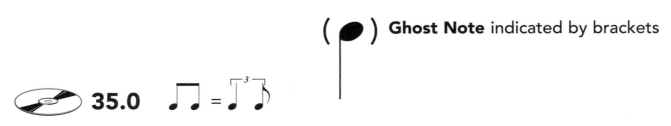

Ghost Note indicated by brackets

35.0

In the following examples, some ghost notes occur on the beat while others occur off the beat. Where and how you use ghost notes can make a big difference to the feel of the music. Listen to the CD to hear the effects produced by the use of ghost notes in various musical situations.

35.1

As with other expressions and articulations, it is a good idea to practice ghost notes with your scales and arpeggios. This example demonstrates the G Blues scale using ghost notes on the beat.

35.2

Here is a musical line which makes use of ghost notes on the beat.

 **35.3**

This example demonstrates the E Blues scale played with ghost notes off the beat. Listen to the different effect produced by using ghost notes off the beat instead of on the beat.

 **35.4**

The ghost note in this example gives momentum to the notes which follow it.

FALSE FINGERINGS

You probably already know that there is more than one fingering for many of the notes on the saxophone (see fingerings index on pages 210 to 213). By alternating between different fingerings of the same note, it is possible to get differences in tone. Listen to the following example which features two different fingerings for the note B♭. The notes played with alternate fingerings have **alt** written above them.

It is possible to find alternate fingerings for some notes by simply playing the fingering for the note one octave below and adding the octave key. This applies to the following notes.

The alternate fingerings for the notes you have just learned can also be used to produce a note a 5th above the previous notes. This is similar to a trumpet player using the same fingering to produce different notes. Practice the following example slowly until you are confident you can produce the correct pitch for each note played with an alternate fingering.

36.   Speak Your Mind   P. Gelling

Here is a solo which makes use of alternate fingerings. At the end of the book you will find a chart which lists alternate fingerings. Go through it and memorize all the fingerings and then experiment with them until you are comfortable using them in your playing.

LESSON THIRTY ONE

BENDING NOTES

One of the great sounds in Rock, Blues, Funk and Jazz is **note bending**. Almost all sax players bend notes, as it is a great way of adding expression to the music. A note can be bent either up or down by tightening or loosening the embouchure. To bend up to a note, start with your embouchure fairly loose as you finger the desired note and then tighten it by applying pressure with your lower teeth until you reach the correct pitch. You will hear the note go up in pitch as you do this. To bend down to a note, start with a tight embouchure and then loosen the pressure with your lower teeth until the note goes down to the desired pitch. It may take some time to become accurate with your bending, but stick with it and your perseverance will definitely pay off. As with other expressions and techniques, you can learn a lot by listening to the way other sax players bend notes and imitating the sounds you hear. In this book a bend is indicated by a **curved arrow** above the note which indicates the direction of the bend. The note written is the note you are bending to rather than from. In other music you may see bends indicated by a crescent shape above the note. In most music however, there are no technique or articulation markings and it is up to the individual player to add these expressions.

37.0

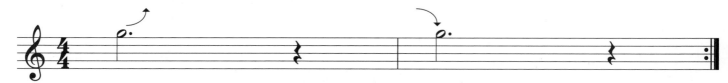

37.1

This example makes frequent use of note bending.

"DIP" BENDING

Another useful bending technique is to bend out of a note, i.e. start the note clearly on the correct pitch and then loosen the embouchure to lower the pitch to an indefinite point to create a "dip" effect which is almost as if you were bending to a ghost note. Here is an example.

37.2

THE TRILL

Another useful musical technique is the **trill**. A trill is a rapid alternation between two notes as demonstrated in the following example. A trill is indicated by the symbol *tr* above the two notes concerned. The first note is often written as a ghost note. Listen to the CD to hear the effect of the trill.

37.3

37.4

Here is a musical line which makes use of the trill. Experiment with trills on different notes. You will find that some combinations are much easier than others, but it is worth developing the difficult ones as well.

THE FALL-OFF

One more useful expressive technique is the **fall-off**. This involves a very fast slurred chromatic run trailing off away from the note you have played. The fall off may go down or up from a note and although it has a definite starting point, it has no definite finishing point. Fall-offs are usually short and can be indicated by a diagonal wavy line moving downwards or upwards away from the original note. It may take some time to develop the ability to use fall-offs. Start by playing short slurred chromatic runs and gradually speed them up. Once again, listen to the CD to hear the effect of the fall-off.

37.5

Here are some musical examples which make use of fall-offs. As with other techniques, try incorporating fall-offs into phrases you already know well and then using them in your improvising.

37.6

37.7

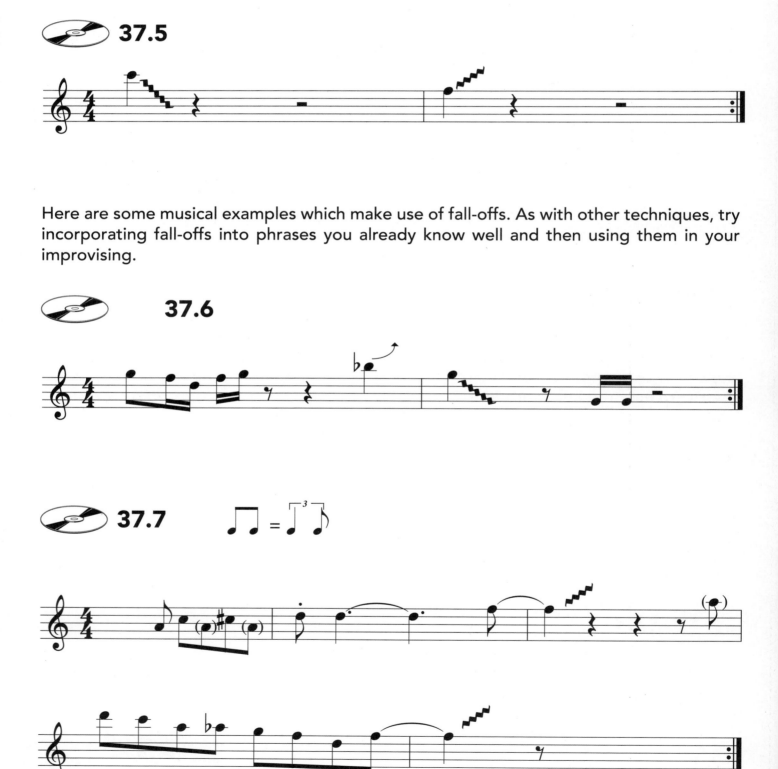

LESSON THIRTY TWO

CALL + RESPONSE

Call and response is sometimes described as a "question and answer" style. It is found in almost all styles of music and originally comes from the Blues. Another common place to hear call and response is in Gospel music where the "call" is made by the preacher and the "response" is made by the congregation. The simplest form of call and response is direct imitation. This is demonstrated in the example below where the guitar (call) is answered by the sax (response). This type of playing is lots of fun as well as being great ear and memory training. On the recording, a space is left for you to play the response on the repeat.

 **38.0**

In the following example, the sax once again answers the guitar, but this time the sax line is a variation rather than an exact repetition. When two musicians play like this it becomes like a conversation, which is very satisfying musically as well as being entertaining for the listener. Try getting together with another musician and playing call and response along with a recorded background. If you are playing the first part (call) make clear statements that are easy for both the other player and the listener to follow. If you are playing the second part (response), make sure your part relates strongly to the call rather than playing a totally different idea. On the recording, a space is left for you to play the response on the repeat.

38.1

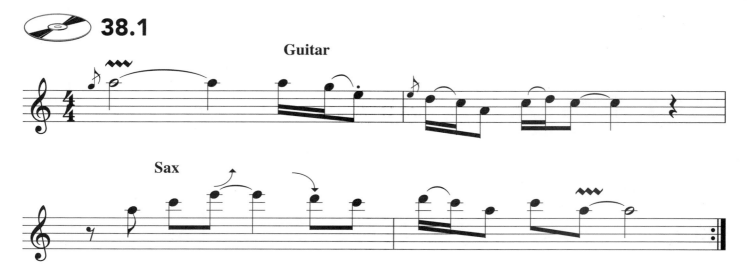

130

One of the most common situations where call and response is used is when you are playing fills in between lines sung by a vocalist. This is demonstrated in the following example. The trick here is learning to play lines that fit well between the vocal lines instead of running over the top of them.

38.2   **Leave This Town Behind**   P. Gelling

One more interesting way of using call and response is between two different octaves or two different ideas on the same instrument, as shown in the following example. Experiment with this type of playing when you are improvising.

38.3

Here is a solo which makes use of almost everything you have learned so far. There are many symbols and markings on the music, which means you can see very specifically how the notes are to be played. Take your time with it and be sure to get all of the expressions, techniques and articulations. Listen to the CD several times until you are confident you can reproduce all of the sounds. As mentioned earlier, most written music doesn't contain this much detail on how to play the notes, so you will need to be aware that any of these expressions and techniques may be used in whatever you are playing. The more you listen to good sax players (both live and on albums) the more you will come to understand and instinctively know where each sound will work and where it won't.

39. Street Preacher

P. Gelling

LESSON THIRTY THREE

MINOR KEYS AND SCALES

Apart from major keys, the other basic tonality used in traditional western music is a **minor key**. Songs in a minor key use notes taken from a minor scale. There are three types of minor scale — the **natural minor scale**, the **harmonic minor scale** and the **melodic minor scale**. Written below is the **A natural minor** scale. The degrees of the scale as they would relate to the major scale are written under the note names.

A Natural Minor

The A natural minor contains exactly the same notes as the C major scale. The difference is that it starts and finishes on an **A** note instead of a C note. The A note then becomes the key note. Memorize both the scale degrees and the pattern of tones and semitones which make up the scale, then play it with your eyes closed, mentally naming the degrees as you play.

Here is a melody in the **key of A minor** which is derived from the **A natural minor scale**. Learn it and then try making up your own melodies based on the ideas presented here.

40.

THE HARMONIC MINOR SCALE

The harmonic minor scale has a distance of 1½ tones between the **6th** and **7th** degrees. The raised 7th degree is the only difference between the harmonic minor and the natural minor. This scale is often described as having an "Eastern" sound.

A Harmonic Minor

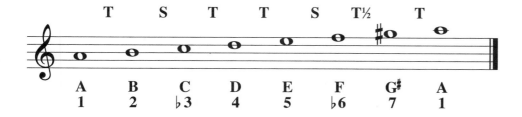

The following example is derived from the notes of the A harmonic minor scale. Once again, learn it and then make up your own melodies from this scale.

41.

THE MELODIC MINOR SCALE

In the **A melodic minor** scale the **6th** and **7th** notes are sharpened when ascending and returned to natural when descending. This is the way the melodic minor is used in Classical music. However, in Jazz and other more modern styles, the melodic minor descends the same way it ascends. An easy way to think of the ascending melodic minor is as a major scale with a flattened third degree.

A Melodic Minor

42.

Here is a melody derived from the ascending melodic minor (Jazz melodic minor) scale.

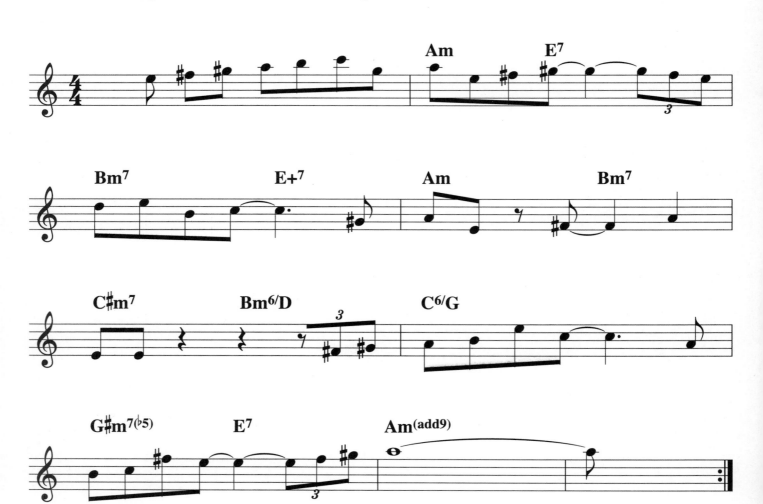

LESSON THIRTY FOUR

RELATIVE KEYS

if you compare the **A natural minor** scale with the **C major** scale you will notice that they contain the same notes (except starting on a different note). Because of this, these two scales are referred to as "relatives"; **A minor** is the relative minor of **C major** and vice versa.

Major Scale: C Major

Relative Minor Scale: A Natural Minor

The harmonic and melodic minor scale variations are also relatives of the same major scale, e.g. **A harmonic** and **A melodic minor** are relatives of **C major**.

For every major scale (and ever major chord) there is a relative minor scale which is based upon the **6th note** of the major scale. This is outlined in the table below.

MAJOR KEY (I)	C	D♭	D	E♭	E	F	F#	G♭	G	A♭	A	B♭	B
RELATIVE MINOR KEY (VI)	Am	B♭m	Bm	Cm	C#m	Dm	D#m	E♭m	Em	Fm	F#m	Gm	G#m

Both the major and the relative minor share the same key signature, as illustrated below.

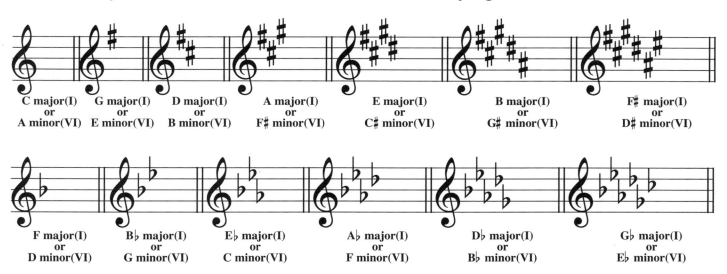

To determine whether a song is in a major key or the relative minor key, look at the last note or chord of the song. Songs often finish on the root note or the root chord. E.g., if the key signature contained one sharp, and the last chord of the song was **Em**, the key would probably be **E minor**, not **G major**. Minor key signatures are always based on the natural minor scale. The sharpened 6th and 7th degrees from the harmonic and melodic minor scales are not indicated in the key signature. This usually means there are accidentals (temporary sharps, flats or naturals) in melodies created from these scales.

136

Here is a popular South American folk song which moves between the keys of **A minor** and **C major** which are relative keys. This melody makes use of both the harmonic minor and the natural minor. Notice the *rit* symbol at the end indicating a gradual slowing down of the tempo.

When playing traditional melodies, many young players think "oh this is easy and boring, I'd rather be improvising". However, a simple melody played expressively with conviction and a good tone can move people a lot more than a fast nonsensical solo. It is easy to cover up musical inadequacies with a lot of fast notes. Listen carefully to the sound you are making as you play the melody and notice any weaknesses in tone, intonation, expression or rhythm which you may need to work on.

43. El Condor Pasa

Here is a piece which alternates between the key of **E minor** and its relative – **G major**. Both these keys share the same key signature which contains one sharp (**F#**). The **D#** note which occurs in this melody comes from the **E harmonic minor** scale. This piece makes much use of arpeggios as well as scales. This piece is not on the CD, but the rhythms are easy, so you should have no trouble reading it. It is written in a Baroque style. The most well known composer from this period is Johann Sebastian Bach, who was a master at writing both melodically and harmonically at the same time. The saxophone did not exist in Bach's time, but one of his famous flute pieces "Siciliano" can be found on page 142.

Perpetual Motion

P. Gelling

LEARNING A NEW MINOR KEY

The process for learning a new minor key is the same as that of a major key, except that there is more than one scale involved. You will need to know the notes of the natural, harmonic and melodic minor both theoretically and on the saxophone. Written below are the notes of these three scales in the key of **D minor**. Learn them from memory and then play the following example.

C Natural minor = C D E♭ F G A♭ B♭
Formula – 1 2 ♭3 4 5 ♭6 ♭7

C Harmonic minor = C D E♭ F G A♭ B
Formula – 1 2 ♭3 4 5 ♭6 7

C Melodic minor = C D E♭ F G A B
Formula – 1 2 ♭3 4 5 6 7

Natural Minor

Harmonic Minor

Melodic Minor ascending

Melodic Minor descending

Once you are confident you can instantly find any note of the scale you are working on, try playing sequences with the notes of the scale, as you have already done with major scales. Work towards memorizing each new pattern and then play it with your eyes closed while visualizing the notation and naming first the notes and then the scale degrees mentally as you play.

It is also important to be able to transpose melodies in minor keys. The process is the same as for major keys - write the scale degrees under the melody notes and then work out what notes those degrees equate to in the key you want to transpose to. Shown below is an example in the key of **A minor** with the scale degrees written under the notes.

Here is the same example transposed to **F minor**. The key signature of F minor contains **four flats**, but the sixth and seventh degrees of the melodic minor are raised, so the notes **D** and **E** will be **naturals**. Remember to learn the notes of the scale first, then work out the scale degrees.

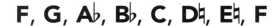

F, G, A♭, B♭, C, D♮, E♮, F

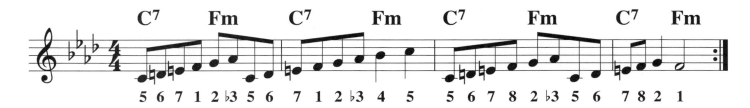

TABLE OF MINOR SCALES

Here is a table which shows the notes of the traditional melodic minor scale in all twelve keys. Remember that the **descending melodic minor is the same as the natural minor**. To work out the notes for the **harmonic minor**, simply **flatten the 6th** degree of the ascending melodic minor.

	T	S	T	T	T	S	T	T	S	T	T	S	T		
A MELODIC MINOR*	A	B	C	D	E	F♯	G♯	A	G♮	F♮	E	D	C	B	A
E MELODIC MINOR*	E	F♯	G	A	B	C♯	D♯	E	D♮	C♮	B	A	G	F♯	E
B MELODIC MINOR*	B	C♯	D	E	F♯	G♯	A♯	B	A♮	G♮	F♯	E	D	C♯	B
F♯ MELODIC MINOR*	F♯	G♯	A	B	C♯	D♯	E♯	F♯	E♮	D♮	C♯	B	A	G♯	F♯
C♯ MELODIC MINOR*	C♯	D♯	E	F♯	G♯	A♯	B♯	C♯	B♮	A♮	G♯	F♯	E	D♯	C♯
G♯ MELODIC MINOR	G♯	A♯	B	C♯	D♯	E♯	F𝄪	G♯	F♯	E♮	D♯	C♯	B	A♯	G♯
D♯ MELODIC MINOR	D♯	E♯	F♯	G♯	A♯	B♯	C𝄪	D♯	C♯	B♮	A♯	G♯	F♯	E♯	D♯
D MELODIC MINOR*	D	E	F	G	A	B♮	C♯	D	C♮	B♭	A	G	F	E	D
G MELODIC MINOR*	G	A	B♭	C	D	E♮	F♯	G	F♮	E♭	D	C	B♭	A	G
C MELODIC MINOR	C	D	E♭	F	G	A♮	B♮	C	B♭	A♭	G	F	E♭	D	C
F MELODIC MINOR	F	G	A♭	B♭	C	D♮	E♮	F	E♭	D♭	C	B♭	A♭	G	F
B♭ MELODIC MINOR	B♭	C	D♭	E♭	F	G♮	A♮	B♭	A♭	G♭	F	E♭	D♭	C	B♭
E♭ MELODIC MINOR	E♭	F	G♭	A♭	B♭	C♮	D♮	E♭	D♭	C♭	B♭	A♭	G♭	F	E♭
ROMAN NUMERALS	I	II	III	IV	V	VI	VII	VIII	VII	VI	V	IV	III	II	I

LESSON THIRTY FIVE

SIMPLE AND COMPOUND TIME

Time signatures fall into two basic categories – **simple time** and **compound time**. **Simple time** is any time signature where the basic beat is **divisible by two**. E.g. in $\frac{4}{4}$, $\frac{3}{4}$ and $\frac{2}{4}$ the basic beat is a quarter note which may be divided in half to become two eighth notes per beat. Any time signature where the basic beat is **divisible by three** is called **compound time**. The most common example of compound time is **six eight** time ($\frac{6}{8}$). Other examples of compound time would be $\frac{9}{8}$ and $\frac{12}{8}$. In compound time, the basic beat is felt as a dotted quarter note which can be divided by three.

THE SIX EIGHT TIME SIGNATURE

This is the **six eight** time signature.
There are six eighth notes in one bar of $\frac{6}{8}$ time. The six eighth notes are divided into two groups of three.

When playing $\frac{6}{8}$ time there are **two** beats within each bar with each beat being a **dotted quarter note.** (This is different to $\frac{4}{4}$ and $\frac{3}{4}$ time where each beat is a quarter note). Accent the 1 and 4 count to help establish the two beats per bar. Here is an example written in $\frac{6}{8}$ time which contains some typical note groupings. This time signature is particularly common in Irish and European Folk music and African music.

44.0

44.1 House of the Rising Sun

This traditional American song is in ⁶⁄₈ time and is in the **key of A minor**. It contains a **G♯** note in bar 14 which comes from the harmonic minor scale, but all the other notes are contained in the natural minor scale. In minor key melodies, it is common to use notes from more than one scale. Don't forget to use the expressive techniques you have learnt when playing a melody even if they are not written as part of the sheet music.

Here is an exercise to help you get familiar with note groupings in ⁶⁄₈ time. Play it slowly with a metronome until you are comfortable with all the rhythms and then gradually increase the tempo. Practice each bar by itself at first if necessary. In the final bar, you will see a dotted 16th note followed by a 32nd note, which is half the value of a 16th note. If you are unsure about this, listen to the CD a few times until you are confident you can play it correctly. Thirty second notes are dealt with in the following lesson.

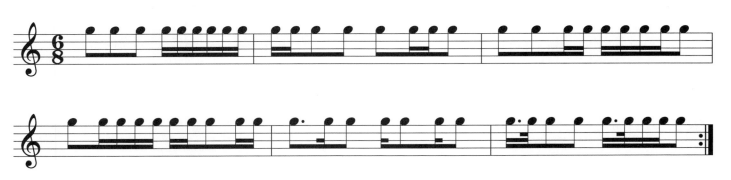

Here is a great piece by **JS Bach** from Sonata number 2 for flute and harpsichord. It is written in the key of G minor in ⁶⁄₈ time and contains several of the rhythms from the previous exercise.

45.   **Siciliano**

J.S. Bach

LESSON THIRTY SIX

THE SIXTEENTH NOTE TRIPLET

Triplets can be created on any note value. A sixteenth note triplet is three sixteenth notes played evenly across the space usually taken by two sixteenth notes. This means that the triplet grouping lasts for the same duration as an eighth note. It is common for two sixteenth note triplets to occur together as a group of six notes across one quarter note beat. The example below demonstrates sixteenth note triplets on one note. As with previous note values, practice it with your metronome and be sure to keep your notes even. To count a sixteenth note triplet, say **ta ka ta**, for two sixteenth note triplets across a beat, say **ta ka ta ta ka ta**.

46.0

ta ka ta ta ka ta ta ka ta ta ka ta ta ka ta ta ka ta ta ka ta ta ka ta

46.1

Here is an example which makes use of sixteenth note triplets.

SWINGING SIXTEENTH NOTES

Like eighth notes, it is possible to swing sixteenth notes by playing the first and third notes of the triplet grouping. Swung 16th rhythms are common in Funk, Hip-Hop and Rock which is influenced by these styles. Swing the 16ths in the following example, and then try some of the earlier examples in the book with swung 16ths.

46.2

 ## 47. Stompin' Down Broadway

P. Gelling

This funky Blues solo uses both swung 16th notes and 16th note triplets. Take your time with it and be sure to get all the articulations and expressions.

TWELVE EIGHT TIME ($\frac{12}{8}$)

Another useful time signature which is common in Blues, Gospel and Soul is **twelve eight time** ($\frac{12}{8}$). In this time signature there are **twelve eighth note beats** in each bar. A bar of eighth notes in twelve eight time sounds the same as a bar of triplets in four four time. Although there are twelve individual beats which can be counted, twelve eight time is usually still counted in four (**1** 2 3 **2** 2 3 **3** 2 3 **4** 2 3) as demonstrated in the following example.

48.0

One of the main reasons for using the twelve eight time signature instead of $\frac{4}{4}$ is that it becomes easier to count when the eighth notes are subdivided. Since there is a number on each eighth note, sixteenth notes can be counted as **+** (**and**) as demonstrated in the following example.

48.1

48.2 So Long Ago

P. Gelling

Here is a solo which makes use of 16th notes in $\frac{12}{8}$ time along with 16th note triplets.

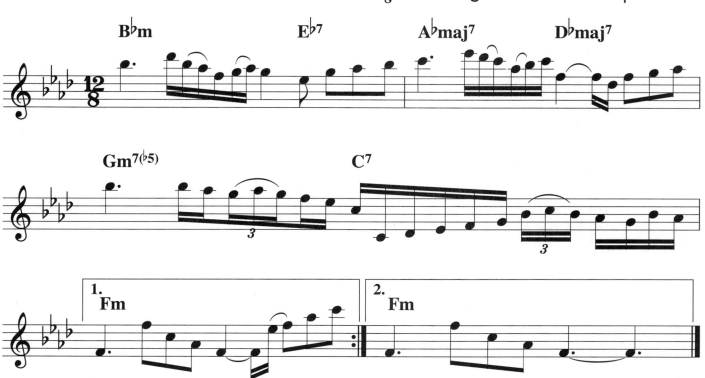

LESSON THIRTY SEVEN

DYNAMICS

The term **dynamics** refers to the **volume** at which music is played. If all music was played at the same volume it would lack expression and soon become boring. Therefore it is necessary to be able to play at a variety of dynamic levels ranging from very soft to very loud. There are various markings for dynamics in written music. Most come from Italian words. Some of these are listed below, along with their English translations. To practice dynamics, play a scale, and then a melody at each of these volumes.

pp pianissimo (very soft) *p* piano (soft) *mp* mezzo piano (moderately soft)

mf mezzo forte (moderately loud) *f* forte (loud) *ff* fortissimo (very loud)

VOLUME CHANGES

Gradual changes in volume are indicated by the **crescendo** (meaning a gradual increase in volume) and the **diminuendo** (meaning a gradual decrease in volume).

crescendo   diminuendo

Learning to use dynamics effectively takes quite a while. A good way to practice dynamics is to play a basic rhythm (e.g two bars of eighth notes) on one note, but at different dynamic levels, ranging from as softly as you can play to as loudly as you can play. Then try the same thing with a short melody. These two extremes are not so difficult, although keeping all the notes consistent when playing very quietly can be tricky at first. Most beginners have trouble making the grades of volume in between *pp* and *f* distinguishable, so be patient and keep practicing until you are comfortable with all the dynamic levels shown above.

Once you are comfortable with different dynamic levels, start adding crescendos and diminuendos. Again, start with one note until you are comfortable with gradual and consistent volume changes, then try crescendos and diminuendos with scales and finally with melodies. An instrumentalist with good control of dynamics and time will always be in demand with other musicians and well appreciated by audiences.

THIRTY SECOND NOTES

Another thing you may encounter in ballads and slow Blues songs is thirty second notes. One sixteenth note divides into two thirty second notes. The example below is shown in $\frac{6}{8}$ time, which is equivalent to half a bar of $\frac{12}{8}$ time. The thirty second notes are counted **1e+a 2e+a 3e+a, 2e+a 2e+a 3e+a,** etc, but are probably best felt rather than counted.

49.

Count: 1 e + a 2 e + a 3 e + a 2 e + a 2 e + a 3 e + a

It is important to be able to move freely between different beat subdivisions without losing your timing. Play the following example **slowly with a metronome** for a short time each day, concentrating on precision of timing until you can do it easily, and then gradually increase the tempo. If you have trouble, practice the rhythms on one note first. Practice playing the whole exercise at a consistent volume, and then vary the dynamics as demonstrated on the previous page.

The following solo is based on the chord progression of House of the Rising Sun. It is in the key of D minor and features the use of 32nd notes. Be patient with it and listen to the recording many times until you are familiar with it.

50. Watching the Rising Sun

P. Gelling

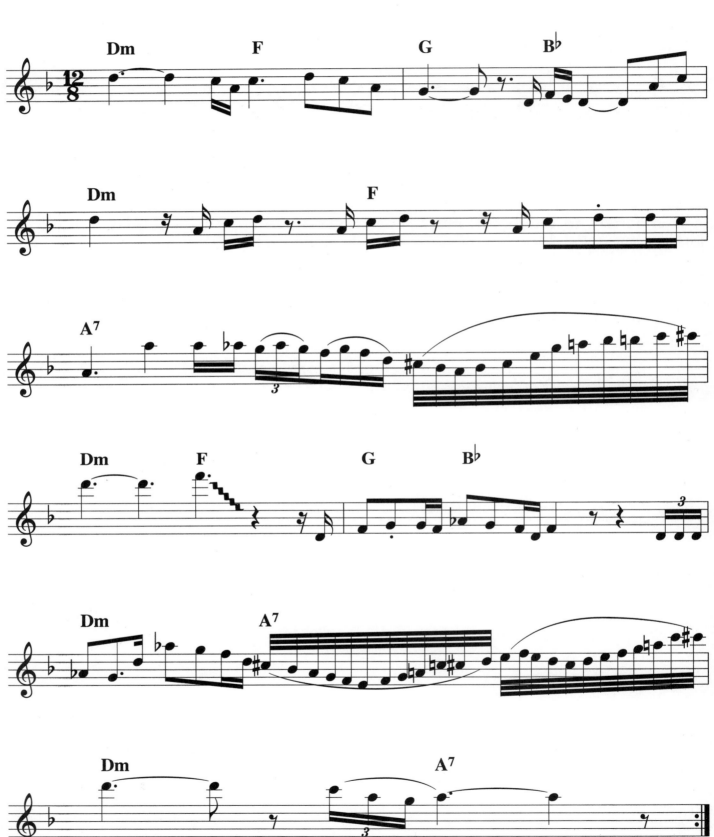

SECTION 3
Understanding Chords, Scales and Modes

LESSON THIRTY EIGHT

MODES

The major scale is probably the most common scale used in music. It is probably the first scale you learned to play on the saxophone. There are many ways of using the major scale, particularly when it is divided into **modes**, which will be the subject of this lesson. To begin with, lets look at the C major scale. As you know, the C major scale contains no sharps or flats. Its notes are C D E F G A B and C again an octave higher. These notes can be used to play literally thousands of melodies in the key of C major. It is not necessary to always start and finish on the note C. Depending on which chords you are playing over, it may sound best to start on **any** of the notes in the scale. E.g. if you were playing over a C chord followed by a D minor chord you could play the scale starting on C for the C chord but start on D for the D minor chord, as shown below. This is a **modal** approach to playing scales.

As well as knowing which notes will sound best over a particular chord, the things which make a melody interesting are the rhythm, the articulations and the order the notes are played in. The scale is only the starting point. If you just run up and down a scale, it gets boring very quickly. Compare the following example with the previous one and you will hear how a melody can be created from the scale.

NAMES OF THE MODES

There are **seven** different modes which can be derived from the major scale by starting on each of the seven notes of the major scale. These modes were first used in ancient Greece and have been widely used throughout history in all types of music. They are particularly useful for improvising or composing melodies over chord progressions. The names of the seven modes and their relationship to the major scale are shown below.

1. Ionian mode – The Ionian mode is another name for the major scale itself.
By starting and ending on the first note of the major scale (C) you can play the Ionian mode.

C Ionian = C D E F G A B C

2. Dorian mode – The Dorian mode starts and ends on the second note of the major scale (in this case D).

D Dorian = D E F G A B C D

3. Phrygian mode – The Phrygian mode starts and ends on the third note of the major scale (in this case E).

E Phrygian = E F G A B C D E

4. Lydian mode – The Lydian mode starts and ends on the fourth note of the major scale (in this case F).

F Lydian = F G A B C D E F

5. Mixolydian mode – The Mixolydian mode starts and ends on the fifth note of the major scale (in this case G).

G Mixolydian = G A B C D E F G

6. Aeolian mode – The Aeolian mode starts and ends on the sixth note of the major scale (in this case A).

A Aeolian = A B C D E F G A

7. Locrian mode – The Locrian mode starts and ends on the seventh note of the major scale (in this case B).

B Locrian = B C D E F G A B

Here is an exercise containing all of the modes derived from the major scale. Listen to the sound of each mode against the chords indicated above the music.

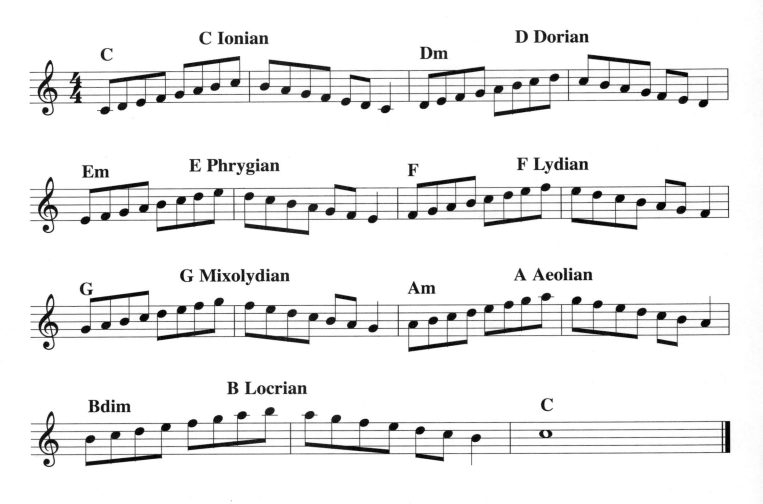

Once you know the notes contained within each mode, it is a good idea to practice them over two octaves wherever possible. The following example demonstrates the **D dorian** mode over two octaves.

MODAL TONALITIES

Even though all these modes are derived from the C major scale, it is possible to create sound from some of the modes which are very different to the major scale. The following example demonstrates a melody created from the **D dorian** mode. This mode is particularly useful for minor key progressions where the IV chord is major, as demonstrated in the following example. Notice that the tonality here is nothing like the a major key even though all the notes are contained in the C major scale. This piece would be described as having a **modal** (in this case, Dorian) **tonality**.

52.0

It is important to practice all the modes with sequences of each interval up to an octave and also to practice improvising with each mode while concentrating on a particular interval. The following example is derived from the **D dorian** mode and makes extensive use of **4ths**.

52.1

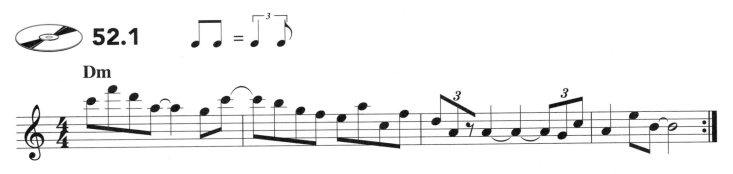

Every mode has its own characteristic sound. Listen to the Spanish Flamenco type of sound produced by the **E Phrygian** mode in the following example. Jazz trumpeter **Miles Davis** makes extensive use of this and other modes on his album "**Sketches of Spain**". Another Miles Davis album which is essential for all aspiring Jazz players is "**Kind of Blue**", which features **John Coltrane** on **tenor sax** and **Julian "Cannonball" Adderley** on **alto sax**. Most of the songs on this album are modal, and feature great improvising by all the musicians.

52.2

CUT COMMON TIME (¢)

This example demonstrates the type of sound produced by the Aeolian mode. This mode is the same as the **Natural Minor** scale and can be used over chord progressions in minor keys. It is written in Cut Common time (¢) which is also called $\frac{2}{2}$ time and represents two half note beats per bar. In this situation, each half note receives one count. Whole notes receive two counts, while quarter notes receive half a count.

52.3

USING MODES IN ALL KEYS

So far you have learnt all of the modes derived from the **C** major scale. Each of these modes can be played in **any key**. Just as there are twelve major keys, there are also twelve possible starting notes for each of the modes. Any note of the chromatic scale can be used as a starting note for any mode. This requires a knowledge of the formula for each mode. The scale degrees of each mode are listed below.

Ionian = 1 2 3 4 5 6 7

Dorian = 1 2 ♭3 4 5 6 ♭7

Phrygian = 1 ♭2 ♭3 4 5 ♭6 ♭7

Lydian = 1 2 3 ♯4 5 6 7

Mixolydian = 1 2 3 4 5 6 ♭7

Aeolian = 1 2 ♭3 4 5 ♭6 ♭7

Locrian = 1 ♭2 ♭3 4 ♭5 ♭6 ♭7

If you are serious about using modes in your playing (and any serious musician should be), it will be necessary to memorize the formula for each of these modes. Don't try to memorize them all at once, take one mode at a time and learn the formula as it relates to the **sound** of the mode and experiment with it. All you need to work out of a mode in any key is the starting note and the formula. Here is the Dorian mode shown in four different keys.

C Dorian = C D E♭ F G A B♭
1 2 ♭3 4 5 6 ♭7

F Dorian = F G A♭ B C D E♭
1 2 ♭3 4 5 6 ♭7

A Dorian = A B C D E F♯ G
1 2 ♭3 4 5 6 ♭7

B Dorian = B C♯ D E F♯ G A
1 2 ♭3 4 5 6 ♭7

A great way to become familiar with all of the mode formulas is to play them all starting from the same note. The following example demonstrates all seven modes starting and finishing on the note **C**. Once you know them in that key, try starting on each different note of the chromatic scale and playing all seven modes. This will take quite some time to master, but by the time you can do it you will be very confident in your knowledge of modes.

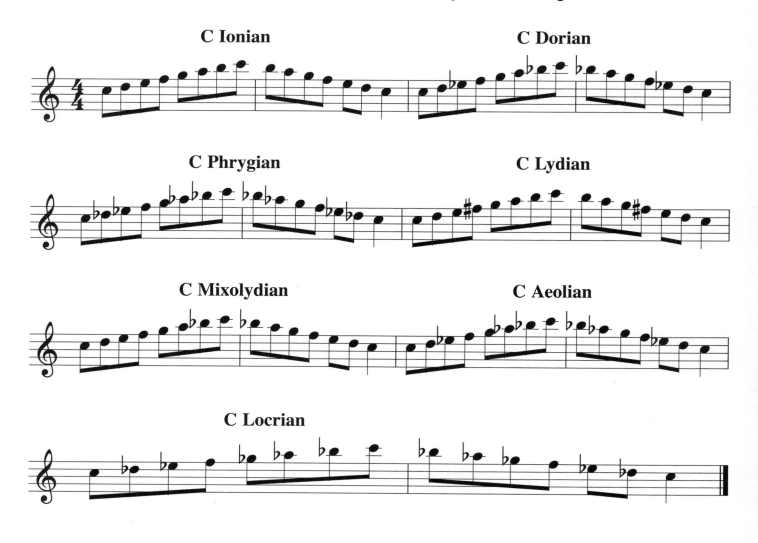

Once you know a mode in a new key, you should begin improvising with it in that key. This next example shows a line created from the **E Lydian** mode.

52.4

LESSON THIRTY NINE

SCALE TONE CHORDS

As well as modes being created from the seven notes of the major scale, it is also possible to create a chord from each note of the scale. By taking the **first**, **third** and **fifth** notes of each mode, there are **triads** (3 note chords) which can be derived from the major scale. Listed below are the seven modes and the triad created from each mode.

C Ionian = C D E F G A B C   **C Major Triad = C   E   G**

D Dorian = D E F G A B C D   **D Minor Triad = D   F   A**

E Phrygian = E F G A B C D E   **E Minor Triad = E   G   B**

F Lydian = F G A B C D E F   **F Major Triad = F   A   C**

G Mixolydian = G A B C D E F G   **G Major Triad = G   B   D**

A Aeolian = A B C D E F G A   **A Minor Triad = A   C   E**

B Locrian = B C D E F G A B   **B Diminished Triad = B   D   F**

Because each mode contains three notes from its corresponding triad, the modes work particularly well when played against these chords. Using modes to play over chords means it is possible to create melodies which are very specific to certain chords. It is possible to use the C major scale freely over any chord in the key of C major, but the C Ionian mode is very specific to the C major triad. If you had a chord progression containing the chords C, F and G you could simply play the C major scale (C Ionian) or you could use the F Lydian mode over the F chord and the G Mixolydian mode over the G chord. Here are some examples.

53.0

Here is a melody using the C major scale (Ionian mode) over the chords C, F and G in the key of C.

The melody derived from the C major scale in the previous example sounds reasonably good but it doesn't fit the chord progression perfectly. Using modes to play over chord progressions means finding the best group of notes to play over each particular chord. Here is the same progression with the **C Ionian**, **F Lydian** and **G Mixolydian** modes played over it. Listen to how well each mode fits its particular chord.

Now try this melody created from the modes in the previous example. Listen to how much better this melody fits the chords than the one in example 53.0 on the previous page.

SCALE TONE CHORD ARPEGGIOS

To be able to improvise well over a chord progression, it is essential to know the notes contained in each of the chords and be able to play them at will. A good way to develop this ability is to memorize the scale tone chords in the key you are working on and then practice various combinations of them. Here are the seven scale tone triads in **C** major played as arpeggios. The ascending pattern in bars 1 to 4 begins on the **root** of each new chord, while the descending pattern in bars 5 to 8 begins on the **5th** of each new chord.

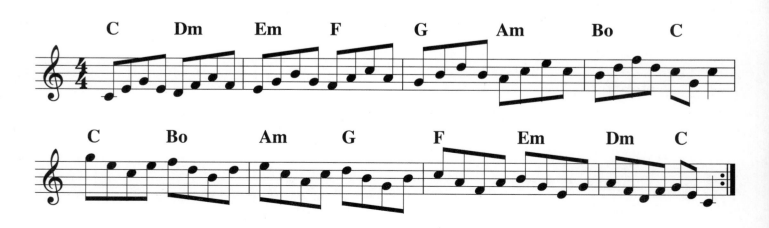

MAJOR KEY TRIAD PATTERN

It is common practice to describe all the chords within a key with **roman numerals**. If you go through and analyse all of the scale tone chords in the key of C major you come up with the following pattern:

I̲	Major	(C Major)
I̲I̲	Minor	(D Minor)
I̲I̲I̲	Minor	(E Minor)
I̲V̲	Major	(F Major)
V̲	Major	(G Major)
V̲I̲	Minor	(A Minor)
V̲I̲I̲	Diminished	(B Diminished)

This pattern remains the same regardless of the key. This means that if you look at the scale tone triads in **any major key**, Chord I̲ is **always** major, chord I̲I̲ is always minor, chord I̲I̲I̲ is always minor, etc. The only thing that changes from one key to the next is the letter names of the chords. This can be demonstrated by looking at the scale tone triads for the key of **G major** which are shown below.

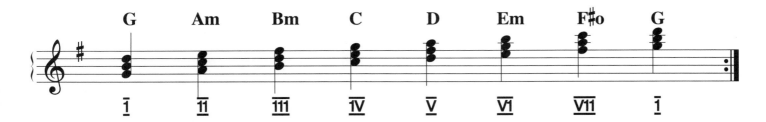

By simply following the roman numerals and remembering which chords are major, minor, etc, it is easy to transpose chords from one key to another. Here is The scale tone triad exercise from the previous page transposed to the key of G major. Once you can play it in this key, **play it in all keys**; both around the key cycle and chromatically ascending and descending across the range of your instrument. Make a habit of doing this with every new thing you learn.

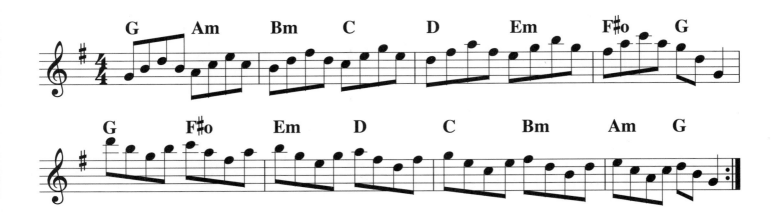

SCALE TONE CHORDS IN ALL KEYS

The chart below lists the scale tone chords in all major keys. However, to become thoroughly familiar with scale tone chords, you will need to write out all 13 major scales and build chords on each of them, being careful to observe the correct sharps or flats for each key. Once you know the notes in each chord of a key, practice them as arpeggios until you have them in your memory.

Summary of Scale Tone Chords

Scale Note:	$\bar{I}$	$\bar{II}$	$\bar{III}$	$\bar{IV}$	$\bar{V}$	$\bar{VI}$	$\bar{VII}$	$\bar{VIII}$ ($\bar{I}$)
Chord Constructed:	major	minor	minor	major	major	minor	dim	major
C Scale	C	Dm	Em	F	G	Am	B°	C
G Scale	G	Am	Bm	C	D	Em	F#°	G
D Scale	D	Em	F#m	G	A	Bm	C#°	D
A Scale	A	Bm	C#m	D	E	F#m	G#°	A
E Scale	E	F#m	G#m	A	B	C#m	D#°	E
B Scale	B	C#m	D#m	E	F#	G#m	A#°	B
F# Scale	F#	G#m	A#m	B	C#	D#m	E#° (F°)	F#
F Scale	F	Gm	Am	Bb	C	Dm	E°	F
Bb Scale	Bb	Cm	Dm	Eb	F	Gm	A°	Bb
Eb Scale	Eb	Fm	Gm	Ab	Bb	Cm	D°	Eb
Ab Scale	Ab	Bbm	Cm	Db	Eb	Fm	G°	Ab
Db Scale	Db	Ebm	Fm	Gb	Ab	Bbm	C°	Db
Gb Scale	Gb	Abm(G#m)	Bbm	Cb (B)	Db	Ebm	F°	Gb

COMMON PROGRESSIONS

One of the best ways to become familiar with chords in all keys is to take a simple progression and transpose it to all of the keys. This may be slow at first, but the more you do it, the easier it gets. Here are some common progressions to learn and transpose. Play through each progression as arpeggios until you are totally familiar with them, as these progressions occur frequently in Jazz standards.

$$\bar{I} \quad \bar{IV} \quad \bar{V} \quad \bar{I}$$

$$\bar{I} \quad \bar{VI} \quad \bar{IV} \quad \bar{V}$$

$$\bar{II} \quad \bar{V} \quad \bar{I}$$

$$\bar{I} \quad \bar{VI} \quad \bar{II} \quad \bar{V}$$

$$\bar{I} \quad \bar{IV} \quad \bar{VII} \quad \bar{III} \quad \bar{VI} \quad \bar{II} \quad \bar{V}$$

HOW TO LEARN A NEW PROGRESSION

Whenever you find a song or chord progression you wish to improvise over, there are several things you can do to help you become more familiar with the chords and which notes will sound good over them. The first step is to analyze the progression in terms of chord numbers within the key (or keys). Just say you hear a progression you like, and a musician tells you it is **I VI II V** (commonly known as a **turnaround progression**). First you need to decide on a key to practice it in. For now, let's choose **A major**. The chords would be **A, F♯m, Bm, E**. Play through the arpeggios of these chords first to make sure you know them well.

The next step is to try improvising over the progression using only these chord tones. Remember that you can move from any note of one chord to any note of the next chord. If possible, approach the first note of a new chord by only a semitone or a tone as this creates a smooth sounding line. Often there are notes which are common to two or more chords. These notes are also good to use at the point of a chord change for the same reason.

It is also essential to know the appropriate modes which work over the chords.

Finally, practice improvising using the modes, being conscious of chord tones at each change.

LESSON FORTY

SEVENTH CHORD TYPES

By adding more notes on top of the basic triads, it is possible to create many other types of chords. The most common types of chords used in Jazz are **seventh chords**. Various types of seventh chords are created by adding another note either a major or minor third above the basic triad. The formulas for the **five basic types** of seventh chords are shown below.

Major Seventh
Chord Formula

Chord Symbol

| CMaj7 |

1   3   5   7

Notes in Chord

C	E	G	B
1	3	5	7

Dominant Seventh
Chord Formula

Chord Symbol

| C7 |

1   3   5   ♭7

Notes in Chord

C	E	G	B♭
1	3	5	♭7

Minor Seventh
Chord Formula

Chord Symbol

| Cm7 |

1   ♭3   5   ♭7

Notes in Chord

C	E♭	G	B♭
1	♭3	5	♭7

Minor Seven Flat Five
Chord Formula

Chord Symbol

| Cm7♭5 |

1   ♭3   ♭5   ♭7

Notes in Chord

C	E♭	G♭	B♭
1	♭3	♭5	♭7

The final type of seventh chord is the diminished seventh. This chord is unusual in that it contains a **double flattened 7th** degree (♭♭7). This note is actually the same as the 6th degree (A) but it is technically called **B♭♭7** because the interval has to be some kind of seventh rather than a sixth because the chord is a type of **seventh** chord.

Diminished Seventh
Chord Formula

Chord Symbol

| C°7 |

1   ♭3   ♭5   ♭♭7

Notes in Chord

C	E♭	G♭	B♭♭
1	♭3	♭5	♭♭7

LEARNING TO PLAY SEVENTH CHORDS

To become thoroughly familiar with the various 7th chord types in every key, you will need to write them out starting on all twelve notes of the chromatic scale (using both sharps and flats). Work on one type of 7th chord at a time until you know them all. It is also important to practice them on your instrument as arpeggios around the key cycle and chromatically up and down.

MAJOR SEVENTHS

A **major seventh** chord is created by adding a **major 3rd** on top of a **major triad**. As with other chord types, learn which notes make up the chord and then practice it as an arpeggio across the range of your instrument as shown with a Cmaj7 chord in the following example.

Once you start to feel comfortable with the major 7th arpeggio, try improvising with it.

Major 7ths Around the Cycle

As with everything you learn, it is essential to be comfortable with major 7ths in every key.

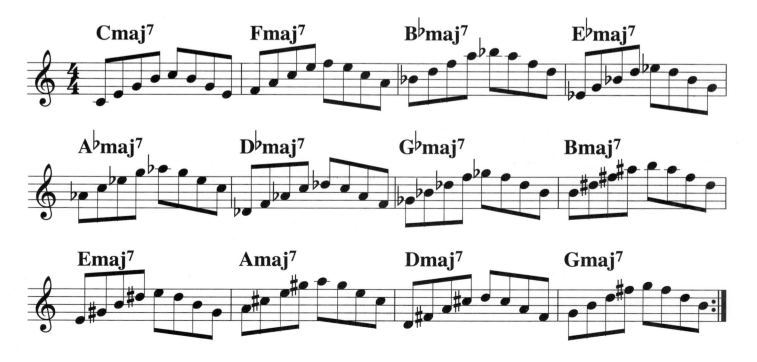

DOMINANT SEVENTHS

You have already learnt dominant 7th chords earlier in the book. It is common to substitute dominant 7ths for other chord types, particularly in Blues and turnaround progressions. Shown below is a Ī V̄Ī ĪĪ V̄ turnaround where all except chord Ī are dominant 7ths. Learn this example and then transpose it to all other keys.

54.0

The following Blues progression contains a turnaround similar to the one shown above. Run through the basic progression first using arpeggios starting on the root note and then try improvising with the notes of the arpeggios as shown in the following example. Learn this solo in the key of **Bb**, analyze all the chord tones and then transpose it to all other keys.

54.1 Seven Seas   P. Gelling

MINOR SEVENTHS

A **minor seventh** chord is created by adding a **minor 3rd** on top of a **minor triad**. The example below demonstrates a **Cmin7** arpeggio.

PRACTICING SCALES AND ARPEGGIOS

When you play Jazz tunes, the root movement of the chord progression may consist of **any** interval between one chord and the next. To be prepared for this, it is a good idea to practice all your scales and arpeggios ascending and descending with all possible intervals. The following example demonstrates **minor 7th** arpeggios **descending in major 2nd intervals**. There are **two sets of intervals** here – one set descending from **C** and the other descending from **B**. Try this practice method with other intervals: e.g. minor and major 3rds.

Minor 7th Arpeggios Descending in Major 2nds

 **55.**

Once you start to feel comfortable with minor 7th arpeggios, remember to practice improvising with them.

MINOR 7 FLAT FIVE CHORDS

The Minor 7 flat 5 (**m7♭5**) is easy to understand because the name itself spells out the chord. These chords are also sometimes called **half diminished** chords. Shown below is an arpeggio of a **Cm7♭5** chord. Once you are comfortable with it, learn it from memory in all keys.

Minor 7 flat 5 chords are most commonly found as a $\underline{\text{II}}$ chord in minor keys. The following example demonstrates a typical use of this chord type.

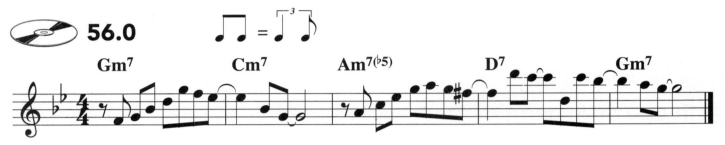

DIMINISHED 7TH CHORDS

The diminished 7th chord is unusual in that it contains a double flat 7th degree (♭♭7). There are three possible symbols for this chord: **o**, **o7** or **dim7**. The following example demonstrates a C diminished 7th arpeggio (**Co**). Since the note **B♭♭** is enharmonically the same as **A natural**, it is written here as **A** to make it easier to read.

Diminished chords are commonly used as passing chords which create tension and then resolve to the next chord, or as substitutes for dominant 7ths chords. In the following example, the **Bo** is a passing chord between chords $\underline{\text{I}}$ and $\underline{\text{II}}$, while the **Ao** is a substitute for $\underline{\text{V}}$.

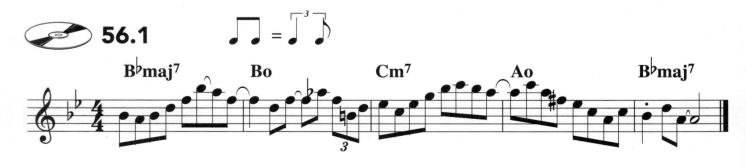

LESSON FORTY ONE

SCALE TONE 7TH CHORDS

By applying the formulas for seventh chords to the C major scale, the following series of chords is created. These are called **scale tone seventh chords**. If you analyze the notes of these scale tone 7th chords, you will notice that they are all based on the C major scale tone triads and each one has another 3rd interval added above it.

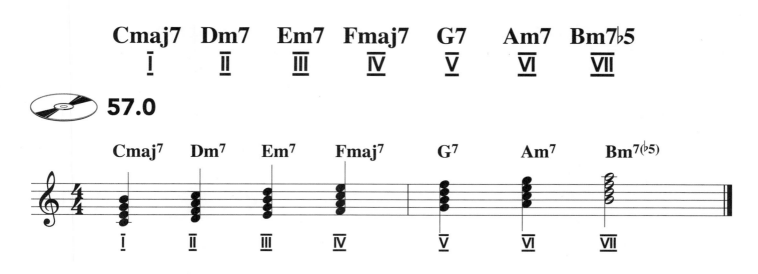

Here are the scale tone 7th chord arpeggios in the key of **C major**. Learn them from memory and then transpose them to all the other keys. It is a good idea to write down the notes of each chord in each key, as this tends to reinforce the knowledge in your mind. If you have trouble doing this, consult the chart on the following page.

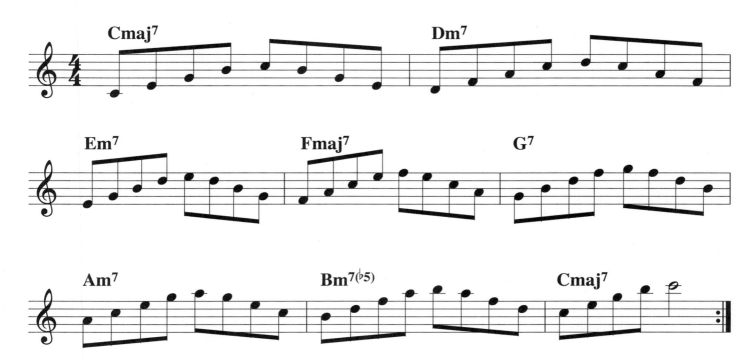

SCALE TONE 7TH PATTERN

Like triads, the pattern of scale tone 7th chord types remains the same for every key. The pattern is summarized below. The minor 7 flat 5 chord is also sometimes called a half diminished chord (ø7).

I	II	III	IV	V	VI	VII	VIII
major7	m7	m7	maj7	7	m7	m7♭5 or (ø7)	maj7

The following chart shows scale tone 7th chords in all keys. If you intend to play Jazz, or any kind of Fusion music, it is essential to memorize all these chords. Work through each key and then take a simple progression and play it in every key. Then try a longer progression, then a song containing the various 7th chord types. The more you do this, the easier it gets.

Scale Tone 7ths in all Keys

I	II	III	IV	V	VI	VII	VIII
Major7	**Minor7**	**Minor7**	**Major7**	**7**	**Minor7**	**Minor7♭5**	**Major7**
Cmaj7	Dm7	Em7	Fmaj7	G7	Am7	Bm7♭5	Cmaj7
Gmaj7	Am7	Bm7	Cmaj7	D7	Em7	F♯m7♭5	Gmaj7
Dmaj7	Em7	F♯m7	Gmaj7	A7	Bm7	C♯m7♭5	Dmaj7
Amaj7	Bm7	C♯m7	Dmaj7	E7	F♯m7	G♯m7♭5	Amaj7
Emaj7	F♯m7	G♯m7	Amaj7	B7	C♯m7	D♯m7♭5	Emaj7
Bmaj7	C♯m7	D♯m7	Emaj7	F♯7	G♯m7	A♯m7♭5	Bmaj7
F♯maj7	G♯m7	A♯m7	Bmaj7	C♯7	D♯m7	E♯(F)m7♭5	F♯maj7
Fmaj7	Gm7	Am7	B♭maj7	C7	Dm7	Em7♭5	Fmaj7
B♭maj7	Cm7	Dm7	E♭maj7	F7	Gm7	Am7♭5	B♭maj7
E♭maj7	Fm7	Gm7	A♭maj7	B♭7	Cm7	Dm7♭5	E♭maj7
A♭maj7	B♭m7	Cm7	D♭maj7	E♭7	Fm7	Gm7♭5	A♭maj7
D♭maj7	E♭m7	Fm7	G♭maj7	A♭7	B♭m7	Cm7♭5	D♭maj7
G♭maj7	A♭m7	B♭m7	C♭(B) maj7	D♭7	E♭m7	Fm7♭5	G♭maj7

Shown below are the seven modes derived from the C major scale played over the seven scale tone seventh chords from the key of C major.

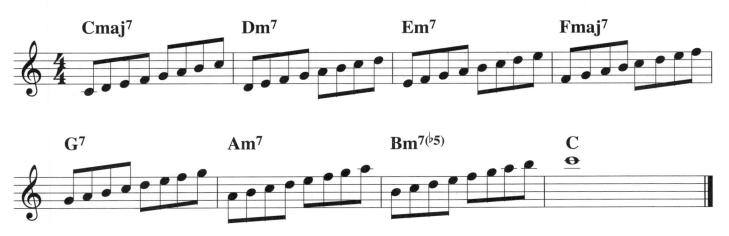

Because each seventh chord contains four notes of the mode it relates to, modes work extremely well over seventh chords. Listen to the sound of this line using the **D Dorian** mode over a **Dm7** chord.

57.1

57.2

Here is a melody which progresses through all the modes in C major over each of the scale tone 7th chords in the key.

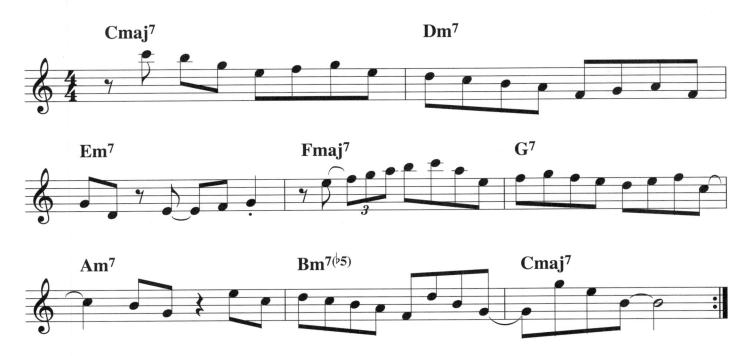

LESSON FORTY TWO

THE Ⅱ Ⅴ Ⅰ PROGRESSION

Once you know how to play over scale tone 7th chords, the next step is to improvise over chord progressions which contain these chord types. One of the most common progressions used in Jazz is the Ⅱ Ⅴ Ⅰ progression. As the name implies, this progression begins on the second chord in the key (Ⅱm7), progresses to the fifth (Ⅴ7) and then progresses to the chord which the key is named from (Ⅰmaj7). A good way to become familiar with this (or any) progression is to have a friend play the chords on keyboard or guitar, or use a play-along CD and play the arpeggios of the chords over the backing. The example below shows this procedure in the key of **C**. Learn it in this key and then transpose it to all the other keys.

Once you are comfortable running through the arpeggios against the chords, try improvising with the arpeggios as shown here. Once again, learn this example and then transpose it to all keys. As stated earlier, this process is essential if you wish to become a good player. You should now be doing it as a matter of course with everything you learn.

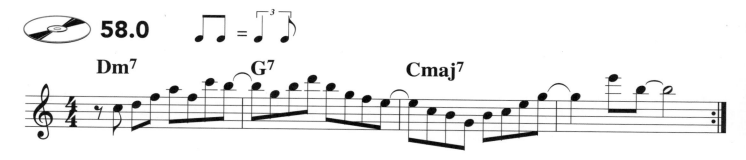

Don't forget to run through the appropriate modes for the progression and then improvising with them. This example demonstrates a line derived from the **D Dorian**, **G Mixolydian** and **C Ionian** modes, being conscious of chord tones at each change.

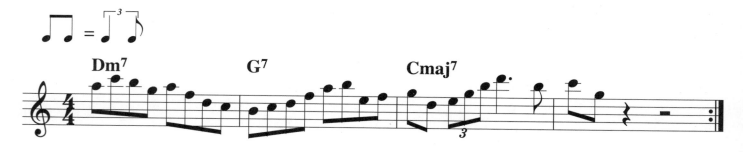

Ï BECOMES ÏÏ

There are many Jazz standards where a ÏÏ V̠ Ï progression is followed by another ÏÏ V̠ Ï progression in a key whose Ï chord is a tone (major 2nd) lower. In this situation, chord Ï **Maj7** of the first key becomes chord ÏÏ **min7** of the next key. This means that if you are improvising over the progression, all you have to do is change the chord from a Major 7th to a minor 7th by lowering the 3rd and 7th degrees a semitone. Here is an example.

58.1

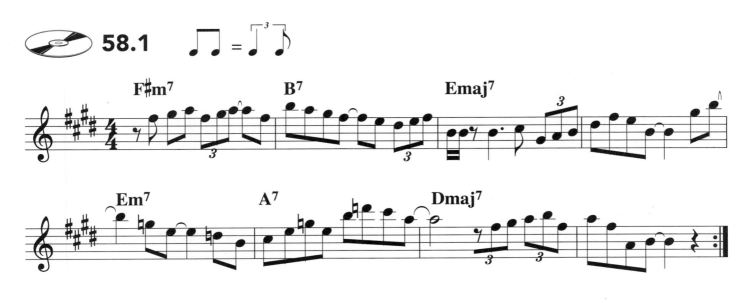

To help you become more familiar with this type of change, it is a good idea to practice alternating between a Maj7 and a min7 chord on the same root note with arpeggios, modes, and improvised lines as shown below.

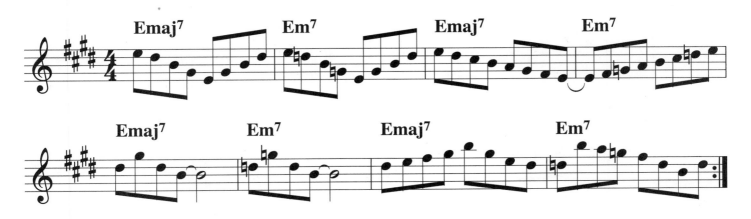

Once you are comfortable alternating between the two chord types, the next step is to repeat the process through all the keys. Try progressing down a semitone until you reach the same note an octave lower, then go up by semitones, then around the key cycle both ways, up and down in major 2nds, minor 3rds and major 3rds.

$\overline{\underline{V}}$ *BECOMES* $\overline{\underline{II}}$

Another common situation is where you have a $\overline{\underline{II}}$ $\overline{\underline{V}}$ progression which does not progress to $\overline{\underline{I}}$, but in the next bar, the $\overline{\underline{V}}$ 7 chord becomes $\overline{\underline{II}}$ **min7** of the next key. In this case, all you have to do is lower the 3rd of the chord by a semitone to change from a dominant 7th to a minor 7th. Here is an example.

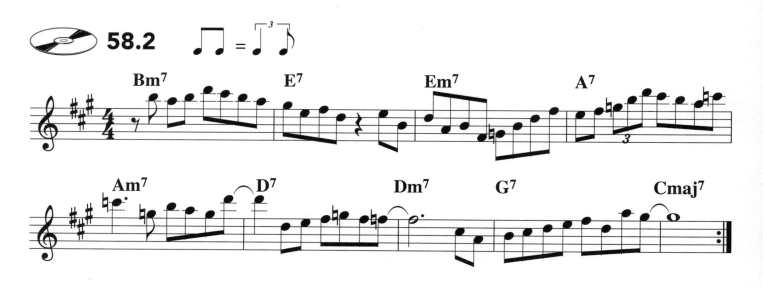

As with the change between the Major 7 and minor 7 chords, practice alternating between a Dominant 7 and a min7 chord on the same root note with arpeggios, modes, and improvised lines as shown here.

Once again, the next step is to repeat the process through all the keys. Try progressing down a semitone until you reach the same note an octave lower, then go up by semitones, then around the key cycle both ways, up and down in major 2nds, minor 3rds and major 3rds.

It is also common for Ⅱ Ⅴ Ⅰ progressions to occur over two bars rather than four. As with the four bar version, practice running through the arpeggios and modes and then improvising with them. Remember to do this in all keys. When you find a pattern you like, play it around the cycle without stopping as shown here. Then play it around the cycle in the other direction, then up and down chromatically through the keys and up and down through various interval cycles.

Ⅱ Ⅴ Ⅰ Phrase Around the Key Cycle

OTHER COMMON PROGRESSIONS

After the $\overline{\underline{II}}$ $\overline{\underline{V}}$ $\overline{\underline{I}}$ progression, the next most common major key progression is $\overline{\underline{I}}$ $\overline{\underline{VI}}$ $\overline{\underline{II}}$ $\overline{\underline{V}}$, or $\overline{\underline{VI}}$ $\overline{\underline{II}}$ $\overline{\underline{V}}$ $\overline{\underline{I}}$. Like the $\overline{\underline{II}}$ $\overline{\underline{V}}$ $\overline{\underline{I}}$ progression, run through the arpeggios of these chords over a backing track of the chords (or better still, practice with another musician and take it in turns to solo or play chords) and then improvise using the arpeggios. Here is an example played over a $\overline{\underline{I}}$ $\overline{\underline{VI}}$ $\overline{\underline{II}}$ $\overline{\underline{V}}$ progression. Learn it from memory and then transpose it to all the other keys.

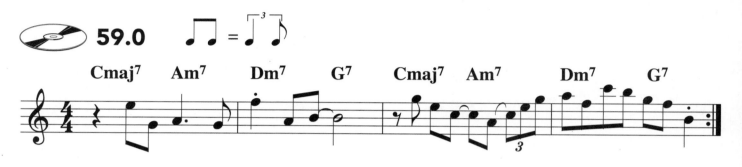

Here is a progression which covers all the chords in a major key: $\overline{\underline{I}}$ $\overline{\underline{IV}}$ $\overline{\underline{VII}}$ $\overline{\underline{III}}$ $\overline{\underline{VI}}$ $\overline{\underline{II}}$ $\overline{\underline{V}}$. As with previous examples, memorize both the progression and the individual notes and learn it in all keys.

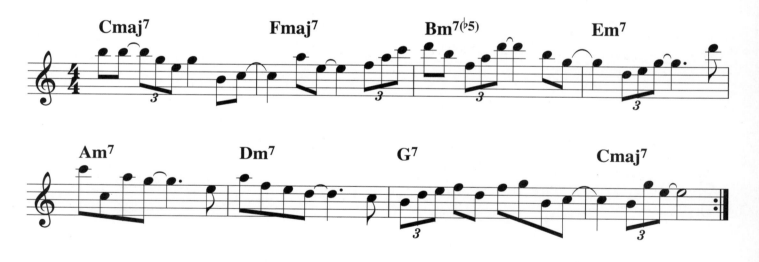

In many Jazz songs, a $\overline{\underline{II}}$ $\overline{\underline{V}}$ progression does not lead to chord $\overline{\underline{I}}$, but to another $\overline{\underline{II}}$ $\overline{\underline{V}}$ in a different Key. Here is an example.

Here is a whole solo making use of short II V progressions moving through several different keys. It is based on the chord progression from Duke Ellington's "Satin Doll". Notice that the eighth notes are played straight rather than swung here. Once you can play the solo, analyze the notes against the chord symbols (all the notes here are chord tones) then transpose it to all the other keys as well as improvising over the progression using both modes and chord tones.

60.   Latin Satin

P. Gelling

LEARNING STANDARDS

It is important to remember that the reason you study chord patterns like II V I's is so you will be able to play freely over the changes to real songs. To learn to play Jazz well, you will need to know lots of popular songs which have become standards. There are many books available which are compilations of standards, often combined with more contemporary tunes. Probably the most famous of these is "The Real Book". Staff in most music stores will know about this book and it is recommended that you purchase a copy, or a similar book and learn the melodies and chord changes to as many standards as possible.

It is also essential to practice improvising over the chord changes to standard songs as often as you can, so that when you get together with other musicians, you have something in common to play. It is important to practice jamming with other musicians regularly, particularly a keyboard player or guitarist who can play the chords while you play the song's melody and then improvise over the changes.

In the Bebop era, musicians began to write their own melodies over the chord changes of popular songs. The chord changes became the standard thing, with melodies being interchangeable. Try learning the chord changes to a song and then writing down your own melody to play over them. The following solo is based on the chord changes to Jerome Kern's "All the Things You Are", which is a popular Jazz standard. This solo makes use of both modes and arpeggios. Analyze the notes against the chord changes and then make up your own phrases based on the ideas presented here. Memorize any phrases you particularly like, and then play them in all keys.

61. Many Things in One

P. Gelling

LESSON FORTY THREE

OTHER CHORD TYPES

By adding more 3rd intervals on top of the various 7th chords, it is possible to create many more chords, notably the various types of 9th, 11th and 13th chords. These will all be dealt with in this lesson, but first there are two more common four note chords worth learning. These are the major 6th chord (usually just called a 6th chord) and the minor 6th chord. These chords are shown below based on the note C.

Major Sixth Chord Formula

Chord Symbol
C6

1 3 5 6

Notes in Chord

C	E	G	A
1	3	5	6

Minor Sixth Chord Formula

Chord Symbol
Cm6

1 ♭3 5 6

Notes in Chord

C	E♭	G	A
1	♭3	5	6

As with previous chord types, it is important to practice the arpeggios for these sixth chord in all inversions and over the entire range of your instrument. Here is an example demonstrating the use of both major and minor sixth chords.

62.0

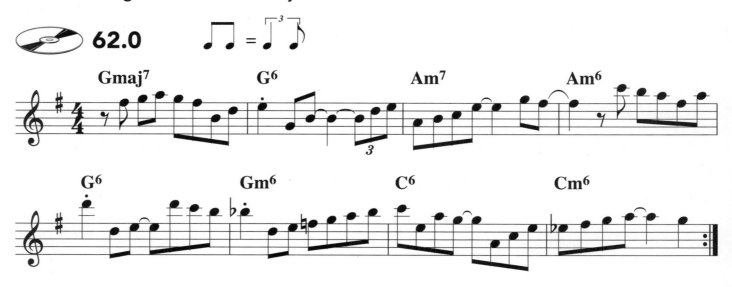

Another chord type you will encounter is the **suspended** chord. In a suspended triad, the 3rd of the chord is replaced by the **4th** degree of the scale, so its degrees are **1**, **4** and **5**. It is also common to add a minor 3rd on top of the triad to create a **suspended 7th** chord. It's degrees are **1**, **4**, **5** and **7**. Since they do not contain a 3rd degree, suspended chords work equally well in both major and minor keys.

Suspended 7th Chord Formula

1 4 5 ♭7

Chord Symbol

Notes in Chord

The following example demonstrates the use of the suspended 7th chord. Notice how these chords resolve to a dominant 7th by lowering the 4th degree back to the 3rd.

62.1

MEMORIZING CHORD TYPES

The more different chords you learn, the more you realize that many of them are quite similar, requiring only a raising or lowering of the **3rd** and/or **7th** degree to create a new chord. A good way to memorize the differences between the various chords is to play arpeggios of all the chords you know in succession from the one root note. Here is an example. Once you can do this easily, repeat the process on each of the notes of the chromatic scale. You should also practice all inversions of the arpeggios, both ascending and descending.

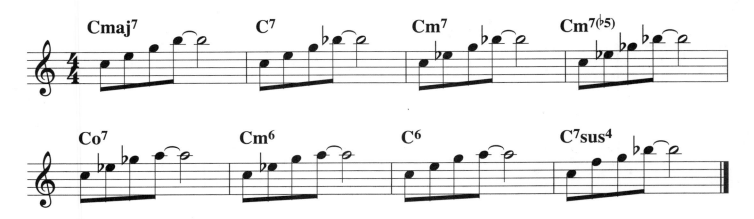

EXTENDED CHORDS

When you play Funk, Jazz, or Modern R&B, you will often find chords which extend past the 7th, notably the various types of **9th, 11th and 13th chords**. These higher numbers come about by repeating the scale from which they are derived over two octaves. Thus, in the higher octave the 2nd becomes the 9th, the 4th becomes the 11th and the 6th becomes the 13th as shown below in the key of C.

C	D	E	F	G	A	B	C	D	E	F	G	A	B	C
1	2	3	4	5	6	7	8	9	10	11	12	13	14	15

As mentioned in lesson 40, most chords are made up of various 3rd intervals stacked one on top of the other. This means that by going through a scale in thirds (i.e. skipping every second note) it is easy to create chords up to a 13th. A **major triad** contains the degrees **1**, **3** and **5** of the major scale. A **major 7th** chord is created by adding the **7th** degree on top of the major triad. This 7th degree is a 3rd above the 5th of the chord. By adding another 3rd on top of the major 7th chord, a **major 9th** chord is created. By adding another 3rd on top of the major 9th chord, a **major 11th chord** is created. If you add another 3rd on top of the major 11th chord, a **major 13th** chord is created. The 13th is as high as the chord can go, because if you add a 3rd on top of the major 13th chord, you end up with the tonic of the chord again.

Depending on the nature of the 3rd and 7th degrees of the chord, 9ths 11ths and 13ths may be either major, minor or dominant in quality. E.g. if you add a **9th degree** on top of a **dominant 7th** chord, you end up with a **dominant 9th** chord (usually just called a 9th chord). If you add a 9th degree on top of a **minor 7th** chord, you end up with **a minor 9th** chord, etc. Written below are the formulas for some typical 9th, 11th and 13th chords.

Chord Symbol

| CMaj9 |

Major Ninth

1 3 5 7 9

Notes in Chord

C	E	G	B	D
1	3	5	7	9

Cmaj⁹

Chord Symbol

| C9 |

Dominant Ninth

1 3 5 ♭7 9

Notes in Chord

C	E	G	B♭	D
1	3	5	♭7	9

C⁹

Minor Ninth

Cm9

1 ♭3 5 ♭7 9

C	E♭	G	B♭	D
1	♭3	5	♭7	9

ELEVENTH CHORDS

By adding another 3rd interval on top of a 9th chord, it is possible to create an 11th chord. Depending on the 3rd and 7th of the chord, you can create major, minor and dominant 11th chords. The chord shown below is a C minor 11th (**Cm11**). By raising the 3rd of the chord from E♭ to E♮ it could be changed to a dominant 11th chord (**C11**). By raising the 3rd and the 7th it could be changed to a major 11th (**CMaj11**).

Minor Eleventh

Cm11

1 ♭3 5 ♭7 9 11

C	E♭	G	B♭	D	F
1	♭3	5	♭7	9	11

THIRTEENTH CHORDS

By adding another 3rd interval on top of an 11th chord, various types of 13th chords can be created. Once again depending on the 3rd and 7th of the chord, you can create major, minor and dominant 13th chords. The chord shown below is a C dominant 13th (**C13**). By flattening the 3rd of the chord it could be changed to a minor 13th chord (**Cm13**). By raising the 7th it could be changed to a major 13th (**CMaj13**).

Thirteenth

C13

1 3 5 ♭7 9 11 13

C	E	G	B♭	D	F	A
1	3	5	♭7	9	11	13

LEARNING NEW CHORDS

It obviously takes quite a bit of time to learn and memorize all the chords up to the 13th in all keys, but if you work at it methodically for a short time each day, you will be surprised at your rate of progress. There is a simple method for learning a new chord group (e.g. 9th chords) or chord type (e.g. dominant 9th chords) and working it into your playing. Start with chords with the least number of notes in them like you have done so far – three note chords first (triads), then four note chords (7ths and 6ths), then five note chords (9ths) then six (11ths) and finally seven note chords (13ths).

First, take the whole chord group and analyze the difference between the various types. The following example demonstrates three different types of 9th chords. Notice that the 9th degree remains the same in each chord. Only the 3rd and 7th degrees change.

Once you have clearly established the difference between the chord types, concentrate on one of them and play it as an arpeggio across the range of your instrument, as shown with the following C dominant 9th chord (**C9**). Notice that the 9th degree is the same as the **2nd** degree of the scale (in this case a **D** note in the **C** mixolydian mode). Even though the 9th is technically an octave higher, you can add this note to the arpeggio in any octave.

The next step is to run through all the inversions of the chord as shown here.

Once you can play all the inversions of a chord, you should know it fairly well. The next step is to improvise with the notes of the chord. The more notes there are in the chord, the closer you will always be to another note of the chord, regardless of what degree you are playing. Unless you are leaping to a distant chord degree for a musical reason (this is quite valid and helps create interest in the line if not done too often), it is usually desirable to create a smooth line by using degrees which are close together.

Another thing worth practicing is playing up through the scale (mixolydian for a dominant 9th chord) to the 9th degree and then back down. By going up to the 9th, you have a chord tone on each beat of the bar both ascending and descending. Next, try ascending through the scale and descending through the arpeggio, then up the arpeggio and down the scale.

Finally, place the new chord you are learning in a context with a chord either side of it and practice improvising over the progression until you are comfortable moving to and from the chord. The following example uses 9th chords and a 6th chord instead of 7ths in a II V I progression.

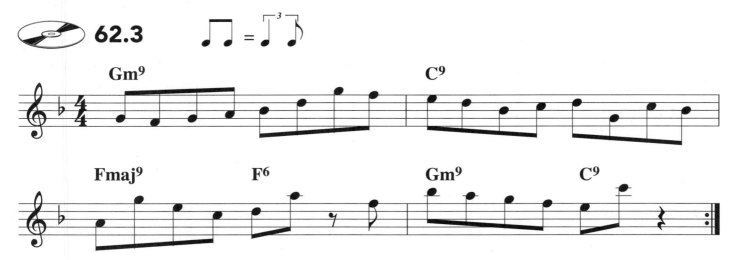

LESSON FORTY FOUR

CHORD SUBSTITUTION

Most Jazz and Fusion players use a technique called **chord substitution** to add different sounds to their playing. Chord substitution simply means substituting another chord for the one written on the page. This is usually done on the basis that the chord to be substituted has **at least one** (but usually two or more) **note in common with the original chord**. To substitute chords successfully, you really need to know your chords well. It is recommended that you purchase a Jazz theory book and study it until you are confident playing any chord, mode or scale in any key without having to think first. It is also a good idea to study this aspect of improvising with a Jazz teacher who will be able to show you some transcriptions of solos by great players which use chord substitution. This aspect of playing can take a long time to become comfortable with, so be patient with it.

SUBSTITUTING TWO AHEAD

The easiest form of chord substitution is to use triads or 7th chords from within the same key as the original chord. In any key you can always substitute the chord two degrees ahead in the scale, thus creating a higher extension of the chord. E.g. Here are the scale tone triads in the key of **C major**.

G	A	B	C	D	E	F
E	F	G	A	B	C	D
C	D	E	F	G	A	B
$\underline{I}$	$\underline{II}$	$\underline{III}$	$\underline{IV}$	$\underline{V}$	$\underline{VI}$	$\underline{VII}$
C	Dm	Em	F	G	Am	Bo

Notice that an E minor triad contains the notes E, G and B. A Cmaj7 chord contains the notes C, E, G and B. Therefore, a Cmaj7 chord can be implied by playing an E minor arpeggio over a C chord. Since the bass or the keyboard is almost certain to be playing the root note, the E minor chord makes up the remainder of the Cmaj7 chord. Scale tone 7ths can be implied for all of these triads by substituting the chord two ahead in this manner. E.g. an F triad can be substituted for a Dm triad, thus creating a Dm7 chord, etc.

Listen to the following example which contains triads two ahead being substituted for the original triad, thus creating scale tone 7ths on every chord. The chord symbols show the triad being played and then a forward slash (/) followed by the bass note which is being played under the triad. Chords notated in this way are called **slash chords**. This is a specific way of indicating the substitution being used (e.g. **Em/C** is the same as **Cmaj7**)

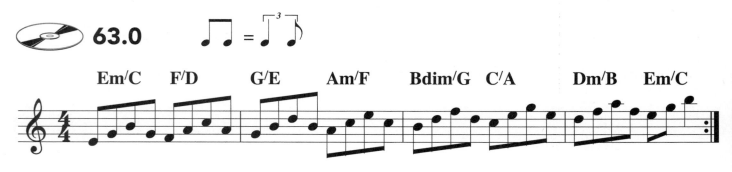

The process of substituting chords two degrees ahead can be continued further by substituting two more ahead and two more ahead until you have covered all the degrees right up to the 13th of the chord. E.g. if you go two degrees further up the scale from E minor, you come to a G triad. It's notes are G, B and D. These are the same as the 5th, 7th and 9th degrees of a Cmaj9 chord. This means you can play a G triad over a C bass and give the impression of a Cmaj 9 chord. Playing an A minor triad over a D bass gives the impression of a Dm9 chord because the notes of the An chord (A, C and E) are the 5th, 7th and 9th degrees of a Dm9 chord. This process applies to all chords within a key as shown in the following example which implies 9th chords for every degree of the scale.

63.1

The reason this kind of substitution works is that the roots of the chords to be substituted go up by 3rd intervals – the same intervals used to create scale tone chords in the first place. The following example shows a Cmaj13 chord broken up into five different triads: C, Em, G, Bdim and Dm. Each of these triads is two degrees ahead of the previous one in the C major scale. Memorize the exercise and then repeat it on all twelve notes of the chromatic scale, mentally naming the degrees and then the actual notes as you play.

By starting on the **second** degree of the scale, you can create chords up to a **min13th** by substituting two ahead. This is demonstrated in the following example which shows a **Dm13** arpeggio made up of Dm, F, Am, C and Em triads.

By starting on the **fifth** degree of the scale, you can create chords up to a **13th** by substituting two ahead. This is demonstrated in the following example which shows a **G13** arpeggio made up of G, Bdim, Dm, F and Am triads.

SCALE TONE 7TH SUBSTITUTION

Like triads, it is always possible to substitute a scale tone 7th chord which is two degrees further ahead in the scale. Shown below are the scale tone seventh chords in **C major**.

B	C	D	E	F	G	A
G	A	B	C	D	E	F
E	F	G	A	B	C	D
C	D	E	F	G	A	B
I̲	I̲I̲	I̲I̲I̲	I̲V̲	V̲	V̲I̲	V̲I̲I̲
Cmaj7	**Dm7**	**Em7**	**Fmaj7**	**G7**	**Am7**	**Bm7♭5**

By substituting Em7 (chord I̲I̲I̲) for Cmaj7 (Chord I̲), a Cmaj9 chord is implied. By substituting Fmaj7 (chord I̲V̲) for Dm7 (chord I̲I̲), a Dm9 chord is implied. This process works for every tone of the scale. Also like triads, it is possible to keep substituting two ahead until you reach the 13th of the chord by substituting Bm7♭5 (chord V̲I̲I̲) for Cmaj7. For each degree of the scale there are three other possible scale tone 7th chords which can be used as substitutions. Over chord I these are I̲I̲I̲, V̲ and V̲I̲I̲. The following example shows the scale tone 7th substitutions for chords I̲I̲, V̲ and I̲ in the key of **C**.

RELATIVE SUBSTITUTION

Another common method of substitution involves relative major and minor chords. Once again, this is because there are notes common to both chords. Cmaj7 contains the notes C, E, G and B, while **Am7** contains the notes A, C, E and G. As you can see, the notes C, E and G are in both chords. This is why these chords work so well as substitutes for each other. The other note in the Am7 chord (A) implies a 13th when played over Cmaj7, while the B note in the Cmaj7 implies a 9th when played over Am7. This process works for **all** relative major and minor chords. The following example demonstrates these substitutions as arpeggios and then an improvised line. Work through this substitution on all 12 notes of the chromatic scale.

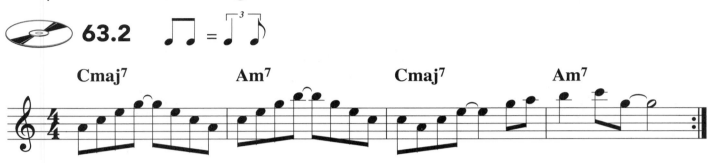

If you are playing with other musicians who understand chord substitution, you may decide to alter the parts played by other members of the group (e.g. bass, keyboards and guitar) as well as the soloist. Then the substitution becomes the standard progression and completely changes the character of the progression itself. This process is particularly useful for making Jazz arrangements of simple popular songs. Shown below is a I IV V progression in the key of C major, along with an alternative version written underneath involving relative minors which may be used as substitutions for the I and V chords. Notice that all the chords have also been extended to 7ths in the second version.

If you analyze the notes of any major 6th chord, you will notice that it is exactly the same as a first inversion of it's relative minor: Therefore, these chords may be freely substituted for one another whenever they occur. In the following example, the saxophone plays a repeated riff using the notes C E G and A while the bass note alternates between C and A. Listen to the CD to hear the effect this creates.

DOMINANT MINOR SUBSTITUTION

Another common form of chord substitution is using chord IIm as a triad instead of chord $\overline{V}7$. Once again, this is because of notes common to both chords. Shown below are a **G7** chord and a **Dm** chord (triad). The notes D and F are in both chords. The **A** note in the Dm chord implies a **9th** when played over a G7 chord. This is called a **dominant minor substitution**.

```
F
D          A
B          F
G          D
V          II
G7         Dm
```

63.4

Listen to the CD to hear the Dominant 9th chord effect produced by this substitution.

Using chord $\overline{II}$ in this manner as a min7 chord instead of a triad requires more care because the 7th degree of chord $\overline{II}$ is the 4th degree of the $\overline{V}$ chord (e.g. a C note in Dm7). This means it will clash with the 3rd of the chord (e.g. a B note in G7) However, this problem can be turned into an advantage by making the 7th of the min7 chord function as a suspension which resolves down a semitone to the 6th, which is the 3rd of the $\overline{V}$ chord as shown in the following example.

63.5

If you analyze the melodic line of the above example you will find that by using the dominant minor substitutions and by having each suspension resolve, you end up with a short $\overline{II}$ $\overline{V}$ progression in each bar, resulting in the following new progression shown by the chord symbols. Write the degrees under each note and see how they make up the chords shown above the notes. Notice also that $\overline{V}$ becomes the $\overline{II}$ of the next bar, changing from dominant to minor each time.

TRITONE SUBSTITUTION

Another common method of substitution is to use a chord whose root is a **tritone** (flattened 5th or augmented 4th) above that of the original chord. This is known as tritone substitution. Like other methods of substitution, the reason this works is that there are notes common to both chords. Shown below are the chords **G7** and **D♭7**. As you can see, the note **F** occurs in both chords. The note **B** is enharmonically the same as **C♭** which is the 7th of **D♭7**, so this note is in both chords too.

$$
\begin{array}{cc}
F & C♭ \\
D & A♭ \\
B & F \\
G & D♭ \\
\mathbf{G7} & \mathbf{D♭7}
\end{array}
$$

In the following example, **D♭7** is substituted for **G7**, creating a II̲ ♭II̲ I̲ progression in the key of **C** instead of a standard II̲ V̲ I̲. Notice how the notes **D♭** and **A♭** in the **D♭7** chord give the melodic line a different flavor to a II̲ V̲ I̲ line using a **G7** chord.

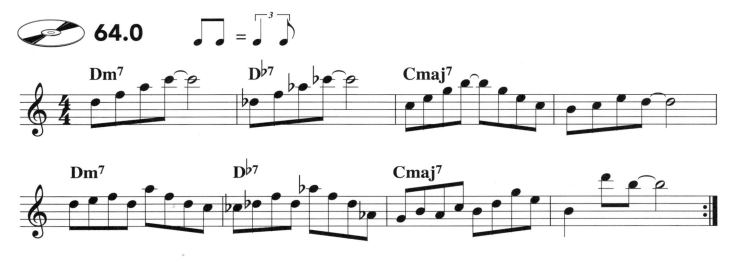

Tritone substitutions are most commonly used with dominant chords, but can be used with any chord type and on any degree of a scale. In some cases, every chord except for I̲ can be a tritone substitution. The following example shows a I̲ VI̲ II̲ V̲ progression and then a second version where ♭III̲ is substituted for VI̲ , ♭VI̲ is substituted for II̲ , and ♭II̲ is substituted for V̲ . This type of substitution throughout the progression is sometimes called **backcycling**. Notice that the chord type has been changed from min7 to maj7 for the E♭ and A♭ chords. This is because the major 7ths contain notes which are common to the key of C.

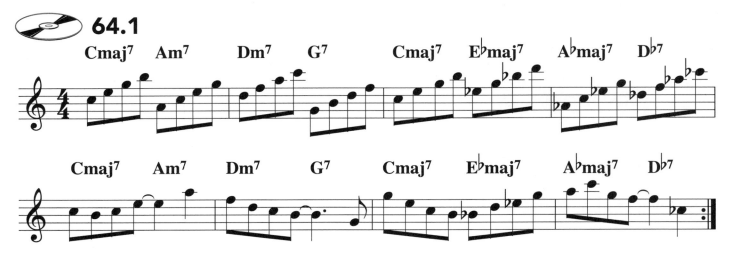

LESSON FORTY FIVE

GUIDE TONES

In any chord, there are certain notes which tell you exactly what the chord is. In major and minor triads it is the 3rd (the 5th is the same in both chords) and in seventh chords, it is the 3rd and the 7th. These notes are called **guide tones**. Shown below are various chords built on a **C** root note, with the guide tones indicated. Notice that these are the notes which change from one chord type to another, while the root and the 5th remain the same.

Guide Tones (7ths) ——————————————→	B	B♭	B♭		
	G	G	G	G	G
Guide Tones (3rds) —→ E	E♭	E	E	E♭	
C	C	C	C	C	
C	**Cm**	**Cmaj7**	**C7**	**Cm7**	

In the following example, the piano plays the notes C and G, while the sax alternates between **E** and **E♭** to indicate a **C major** chord and then a **C minor** chord.

65.0

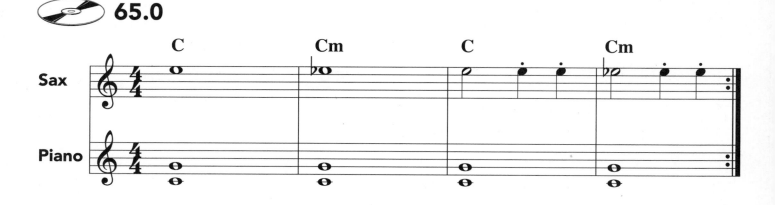

In this example, both the 3rd and the 7th are used as guide tones to indicate the chord types.

65.1

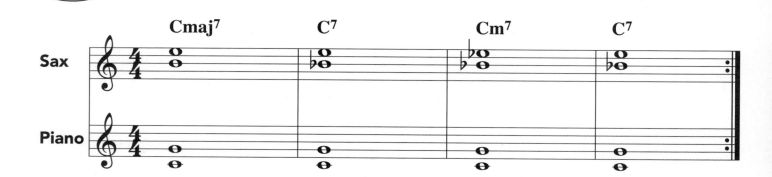

PRACTICAL USE OF GUIDE TONES

There are several ways in which guide tones are commonly used. They can be played by two or more players as a horn section backing a soloist or vocalist. They can also be used by a single player to create a counter line while the melody is being played, or they can be used as a guide to the smoothest way through a progression when improvising. When using the guide tones as a basis for an improvised line, the soloist often plays a guide tone right on each chord change. The following example shows two guide tone lines for $\overline{\text{II}}$ $\overline{\text{V}}$ $\overline{\text{I}}$ progressions. Notice how the 3rd of one chord becomes the 7th of the next chord and vice versa. In the first half, the 7th is above the 3rd, while in the second half, they are reversed. The choice of which note is on top is up to the players, depending on the musical context.

65.2

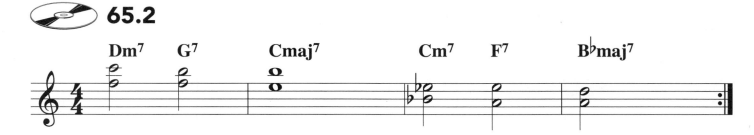

Guide tones are extremely useful when writing a song arrangement, as they make for economical writing. E..g. the bass will usually play the root of a chord, so there is no need for a two part horn section to repeat that note. The 5th doesn't indicate major, minor or dominant chord quality, so it can also be left out. The horn players can play the essential notes only, which are the 3rd and the 7th. Of course, the notes chosen depend on the musical context, as other group members (e.g. keyboard or guitar) may already have these notes allocated to their part, and in some situations a busier unison or octave line may be more effective than guide tones.

The following example is a two part Funk line using the guide tones of the chords **C7** (**E** and **B♭**), **F7** (**E♭** and **A**), and **G7** (**F** and **B**). These are chords $\overline{\text{I}}$, $\overline{\text{IV}}$ and $\overline{\text{V}}$ in the **key of C** played as dominants – as in a Blues. The part is created by simply playing the guide tones and adding a rhythm which works in the musical context.

65.3

An effective way of varying a guide tone based part (or a full chord) is to approach it from a semitone below or to deviate from the chord temporarily by a semitone in either direction before returning to the chord tones. Here is an example based on the previous part.

As mentioned earlier, guide tones can also be used as a framework for improvisation. The following example shows how this can be done over a II V I progression. The guide tones are played right on the point of each chord change, with notes from the appropriate mode being used as the other notes over each chord. Write out the two lines of guide tones for this progression and then analyze the line against them. Then memorize both this line and the basic guide tone lines and transpose them to every other key. The more familiar you are with the guide tone lines for any progression, the easier you will be able to improvise over it.

65.5

OTHER GUIDE TONES

Although the 3rd and 7th of a chord are the most common guide tones, there are other notes in various types of chords which can be important in indicating the particular chord type. In triads, this can be the **5th**, which can indicate a diminished or augmented chord when combined with the 3rd of the chord. In the following example, the piano in the first two bars plays a C root note and a minor 3rd (Eb) while the saxophone alternates between the 5th (G) and the flat 5th (Gb) to indicate first a minor chord and then a diminished chord.

In the third and fourth bars, the piano plays the C root note and a major 3rd (E) while the sax alternates between the 5th (G) and the sharp 5th (G#) to indicate first a major chord and then an augmented chord.

66.0

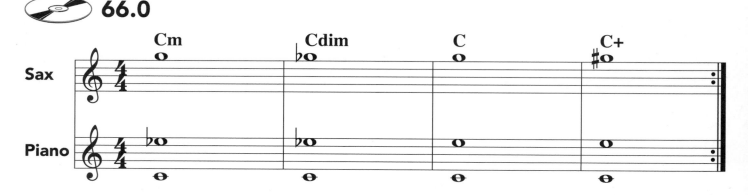

66.1

In **6th chords**, the **6th degree** is a guide tone as demonstrated in the following example.

All the upper extensions of a chord (9ths, 11ths and 13ths) can also be used as guide tones as shown in the following example. Notice that the 13th degree is the same as the 6th. However, the presence of the 7th degree in the chord tells you that it is a 13th because in a 6th chord, the 6th degree is used instead of the 7th.

66.2

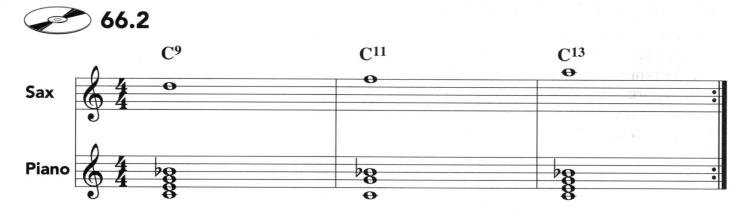

The more notes there are in a chord, the more possible guide tones it contains. In a seventh chord, there are two but anything higher contains three. The fact that there are more guide tones can make it easier to create a smooth line between chord changes. In the following example, the sax plays one note (**G**) while the chords change under it. This note begins as the 3rd of Ebmaj7, then becomes the 4th of Dsus7, then the 9th of F9, and finally the 13th of Bb13.

66.3

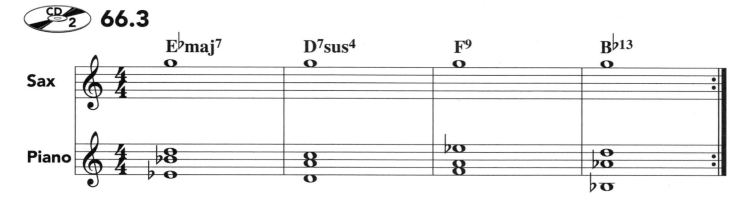

GUIDE TONES IN MODES

Like chords, it is also possible to identify modes by certain notes contained in them. The 3rd identifies whether a mode belongs to a major or minor group, but other notes narrow the possibilities even further. E.g. The only difference between the Ionian and Mixolydian modes is that the Ionian contains a natural 7th, while the Mixolydian contains a flattened 7th. Shown below are the notes which identify each mode. This becomes easy to understand if you play through all the modes starting from the same note.

Ionian	♮3 ♮7				C Ionian	C	D	E	F	G	A	B	C
Dorian	♭3 ♮6 ♭7				C Dorian	C	D	E♭	F	G	A	B♭	C
Phrygian	♭2 ♭3 ♭6 ♭7				C Phrygian	C	D♭	E♭	F	G	A♭	B♭	C
Lydian	♯4				C Lydian	C	D	E	F♯	G	A	B	C
Mixolydian	♭7				C Mixolydian	C	D	E	F	G	A	B♭	C
Aeolian	♭3 ♭6 ♭7				C Aeolian	C	D	E♭	F	G	A♭	B♭	C
Locrian	♭2 ♭3 ♭5 ♭6 ♭7				C Locrian	C	D♭	E♭	F	G♭	A♭	B♭	C

LESSON FORTY SIX

ALTERED CHORDS

A common variation on all of the basic chord types is the use of **altered chords.** As shown in the previous lesson, these can be derived from minor scales when they are harmonized. The flattening or raising of 3rds and 7ths is common in basic chord construction, but the other degrees of a chord may also be raised or lowered. The most common altered chords involve alterations to the **5th** and/or the **9th.** Usually the alteration appears in the name of the chord. Some examples are given below.

Seven Flat Five Chord Formula

Chord Symbol

C7♭5

1   3   ♭5   ♭7

Notes in Chord

C	E	G♭	B♭
1	3	♭5	♭7

Seven Sharp Nine Chord Formula

Chord Symbol

C7♯9

1   3   5   ♭7   ♯9

Notes in Chord

C	E	G	B♭	D♯
1	3	5	♭7	♯9

Thirteenth Sharp Five, Flat Nine

Chord Symbol

C7♯5♭9

1   3   ♯5   ♭7   ♭9   11   13

Notes in Chord

C	E	G♯	B♭	D♭	F	A
1	3	♯5	♭7	♭9	11	13

Although alterations can be made to any chord, the most common altered chords are **dominants**, e.g. the $\overline{\text{V}}$7 in a $\overline{\text{II}}$ $\overline{\text{V}}$ $\overline{\text{I}}$ progression. Here is an example using a **7♯5** chord (also called an augmented 7th e.g. **F+7**). Listen to how the raised 5th adds a different flavor to the line.

LEARNING ALTERED CHORDS

Altered chords can be learnt in the same manner as any other chord types. First, learn the degrees of the chord and then practice the basic arpeggio in all keys until you are comfortable with the sound of it. Then play all the inversions of the arpeggio across the range of your instrument, then improvise with the notes of the chord, and finally, practice improvising with the chord in a context (e.g. as the dominant chord in a $\overline{\text{II}}$ $\overline{\text{V}}$ $\overline{\text{I}}$ progression.) The following example demonstrates an arpeggio of a **C7♭5♭9** chord and then an improvised line using the notes of the chord.

This example makes use of the previous chord along with other altered chords. Notice the use of major and minor 9th chords here also.

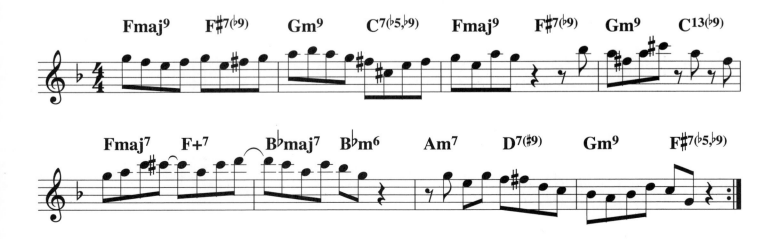

SHARP ELEVEN CHORDS (♯11)

When playing 11th chords, a particular problem arises because the 11th degree is the same as the 4th and this clashes with the 3rd of the chord which is only a semitone distant. This it particularly noticeable when the chord played by a harmonic instrument is in the same register as the melody player's 11th.

When playing suspended triads and seventh chords, the 4th replaces the 3rd, so there is no clash. However, when playing 11th or 13th chords, the **11th** degree is either **sharpened by a semitone**, or omitted from the chord. In minor chords, the 11th does not need altering, because it is already a whole tone away from the flattened 3rd degree and therefore doesn't clash as much. The following example demonstrates the sound of major and dominant **13♯11** chords.

Here is an improvised line created from the notes of these two chord types.

Now try this progression which uses ♯11 chords amongst other chord types.

LESSON FORTY SEVEN

HARMONIZING MINOR SCALES

By placing rows of 3rd intervals above minor scales, chords are created in the same manner as they are when harmonizing major scales. However, because of the different sequences of tones and semitones in the harmonic and melodic minors, some of these chords will be different to those in major keys. Shown below is an A natural minor scale harmonized as 7th chords. Notice that the chords are exactly the same as those contained in the key of C major. The only difference is the starting and finishing point. Because the minor scale starts on **A**, A minor will now be chord $\underline{I}$ instead of $\underline{VI}$.

	G	A	B	C	D	E	F
	E	F	G	A	B	C	D
	C	D	E	F	G	A	B
	A	B	C	D	E	F	G
	$\underline{I}$	$\underline{II}$	$\underline{III}$	$\underline{IV}$	$\underline{V}$	$\underline{VI}$	$\underline{VII}$
Natural Minor	Am7	Bm7♭5	Cmaj7	Dm7	Em7	Fmaj7	G7

If you harmonize the harmonic or melodic minor scale, the chords will not be identical to those of the relative major. Shown below is the A harmonic minor harmonized as 7th chords. The raised 7th degree results in different chord types for chords $\underline{I}$ (a minor chord with a major 7th: **m/maj7**), $\underline{III}$, (a major 7th chord with a raised 5th: **maj7♯5**), $\underline{V}$ (a dominant 7th chord) and $\underline{VII}$ (a diminished 7th chord).

	G♯	A	B	C	D	E	F
	E	F	G♯	A	B	C	D
	C	D	E	F	G♯	A	B
	A	B	C	D	E	F	G♯
	$\underline{I}$	$\underline{II}$	$\underline{III}$	$\underline{IV}$	$\underline{V}$	$\underline{VI}$	$\underline{VII}$
Harmonic Minor	Am/maj7	Bm7♭5	Cmaj7♯5	Dm7	E7	Fmaj7	G♯°7

By harmonizing the ascending melodic minor scale, even more of the chords are altered. As you can see from the table below, none of the chords here are the same as those derived from the natural minor. The fact that there are three different minor scales gives you many chord options for harmonizing a melody in a minor key. This is discussed on the following page.

	G♯	A	B	C	D	E	F♯
	E	F♯	G♯	A	B	C	D
	C	D	E	F♯	G♯	A	B
	A	B	C	D	E	F♯	G♯
	$\underline{I}$	$\underline{II}$	$\underline{III}$	$\underline{IV}$	$\underline{V}$	$\underline{VI}$	$\underline{VII}$
Melodic Minor	Am/maj7	Bm7	Cmaj7♯5	D7	E7	F♯m7♭5	G♯m7♭5

MINOR KEY PROGRESSIONS

Although there are many options for harmonizing minor key melodies, there are certain chord choices which are more common than others. The most common II̲ V̲ I̲ progression in a minor key is made up of a II̲m7♭5, a V̲7 and a I̲m7. The I̲ comes from the natural minor, the V̲ comes from the harmonic minor and the II̲ can be created from either scale. Shown below are two minor key II̲ V̲ I̲ progressions with chord arpeggios and then improvised lines played over them using the chord tones.

69.0

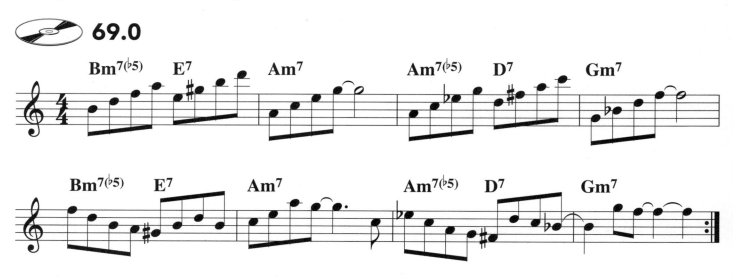

Another common practice in minor keys is to have a minor triad as the I chord with a line of guide tones either above, below, or running through the chord voicing, resulting in various changes to the overall chord. In the following example, notice that only the upper guide tones are needed to create the various **A minor** chords.

69.1

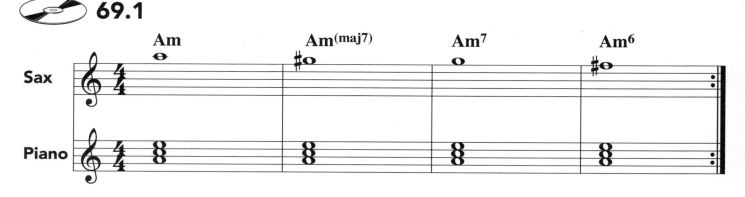

69.2

Here is an example which uses the above guide tone line and extends it further to include all the chords. Analyze the line against the chords and then transpose it to all the other keys.

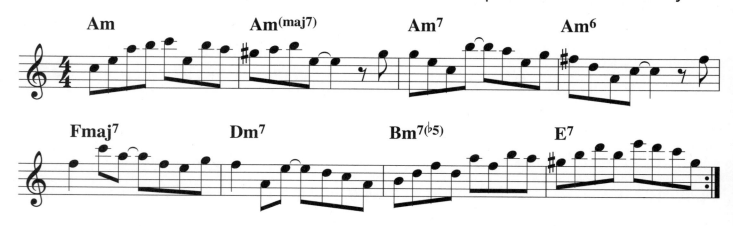

MINOR KEY MODES

Like the major scale, it is possible to derive seven different modes from each of the three types of minor scales. Modes derived from the natural minor will be identical to those derived from it's relative major. However, harmonic and ascending melodic minor scales produce entirely different sets of modes because of the raised 7th and 6th degrees contained in them. The example below shows the seven modes derived from a C harmonic minor scale. Notice how they work over the scale tone chords from the key of C minor shown above each mode.

C Harmonic Minor Modes

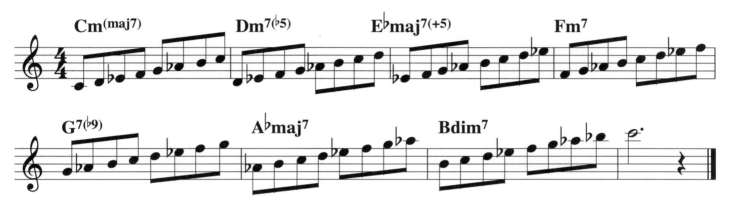

When improvising in minor keys, you will be able to create lines which best fit the progression if you use the modes from the scale which the chords were derived from. Here is a II̲ V̲ I̲ progression in C minor which makes use of the modes shown for these chords in the previous example.

Here are the modes derived from a C melodic minor scale. Once again, listen to how each one works with the scale tone chord it is played over.

C Melodic Minor Modes

HIGHER EXTENSIONS IN MINOR KEYS

Like major scale tone chords, it is possible to add 9ths, 11ths and 13ths to chords built on the notes of minor scales. Shown below are scale tone 9th chords built on an A harmonic minor scale. Notice that some of the chords are no longer straight minor, dominant or major 9ths, but have more complex names because of the alterations caused by the raised 7th degree of the harmonic minor scale (in this case, a **G♯** note). These chords may seem confusing at first and may take a while to learn, but in the long run it is well worth it, as knowledge of these chords will help you improvise better and more easily in minor keys.

	B	C	D	E	F	G♯	A
	G♯	A	B	C	D	E	F
	E	F	G♯	A	B	C	D
	C	D	E	F	G♯	A	B
	A	B	C	D	E	F	G♯
	I̲	I̲I̲	I̲I̲I̲	I̲V̲	V̲	V̲I̲	V̲I̲I̲
Harmonic Minor	Am9/maj7	Bm7♭5♭9	Cmaj9♯5	Dm9	E7♭9	Fmaj7♯9	G♯m6/9♭5

When harmonizing melodies in minor keys, some of the higher extensions are more commonly used than others. The most common is the use of the ♭**9** in chord V̲. The following example demonstrates the use of this note in a minor I̲I̲ V̲ I̲ progression.

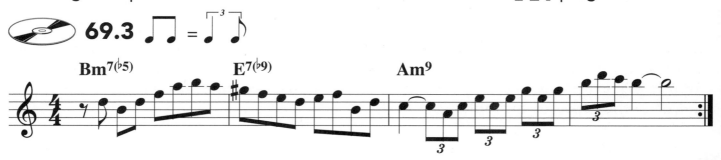

SUBSTITUTIONS IN MINOR KEYS

All the types of substitution you learnt in major keys (relative substitutions, scale tone triads or 7ths two degrees ahead in the key, dominant minor, and tritone substitutions) can be applied to minor keys as well. The main difference you will find is that when you start to go into the upper extensions of chords built on the harmonic and melodic minors, you will get alterations to the chords. Shown below are the chords resulting from substituting scale tone 7th chords two ahead for the standard scale tone 7ths of **A melodic minor**.

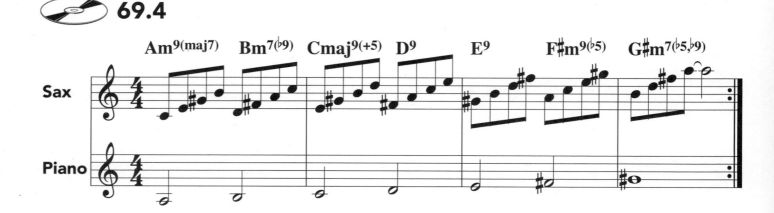

Here is a solo based on the progression to "Black Orpheus" by Louis Bonfa. It is in the key of B minor and makes use of some of the new chords you have learnt. It also contains a section in D major which is the relative of B minor. Learn the solo, analyze it and then transpose it to all twelve keys.

70. Amazon Breeze

C. Soole

LESSON FORTY EIGHT

LEARNING SONG FORMS

With all the arpeggios and scales you have learned, along with your instrumental and musical techniques, you now have all the knowledge you need to become a great player. The important thing is to use your knowledge and technique regularly in musical situations. By now you should be playing with other musicians as often as possible as well as performing live. You should also be playing along with albums every day, sometimes copying what you hear and sometimes improvising, as well as transcribing solos by your favorite players and analyzing them in terms of note choices and use of rhythm.

To play with other musicians, you will need to know lots of songs. Get a good fake book with a large collection of standards and start learning both the melody and chord changes to as many songs as you can. Make a habit of memorizing them and then transposing them to all keys. As you learn more songs, you will find that there are certain progressions which come up regularly, the most common being $\overline{\text{II}}$ $\overline{\text{V}}$ $\overline{\text{I}}$. If you play with Jazz musicians, there are certain song forms which they will assume you know from memory. These include "**Rhythm Changes**" (a chord progression based on George Gershwin's "I Got Rhythm") and several variations on the **12 bar Blues** form. Both these will be discussed in this lesson.

Rhythm Changes are a typical example of **32 bar Song Form**, or **AABA form**. This form **consists of an** A **section played twice**, followed by a **B section** (called a **bridge**) and then a return to the **A section** or sometimes a variation of the A section. There are literally thousands of songs which use the **AABA** form.

PLAY-ALONG RECORDINGS

A great way to become familiar with the form of a song is to use a play-along recording of it. There are many **play along recordings** available which feature a rhythm section but no melody instrument. Many of them contain either Standard songs or progressions which are very much like particular Standards. You can watch the melody and chord progression in a book as you listen to the recording and then play the melody of the song along with the rhythm section. Once you are comfortable doing that, you can start improvising solos over the form until you are comfortable with it. By the time you can do this, you are ready to play the song with other musicians.

JAZZ TERMINOLOGY

Here are some terms which you will need to be familiar with if you intend to play Jazz.

Tune - A song or composition which is used as the basis for improvisation.
Changes - The underlying chord progression of a song (a series of chord changes).
Head - The melody of a song, usually played at the start and finish, with solos in between.
Chorus - Once through the entire form of the piece.
Bridge - The B Section or "middle eight".
Blowing - Improvising, taking a solo.
Trading Fours - Musicians taking turns to improvise four bar phrases.
Bop - Bebop style (e.g. Charlie Parker, Dizzy Gillespie, Thelonious Monk).

There are many more such terms, but knowing these will help you out in Jam sessions.

RHYTHM CHANGES

As mentioned on the previous page, the term "Rhythm Changes" means a progression based on a song by George Gershwin called I Got Rhythm. Over the years there have been many new melodies (or **"heads"** in Jazz terms) written on this progression and is still routinely used by musicians jamming together or auditioning a new band member. The following example shows the basic progression in the key of **C**. On the CD it is played without a melody. Try improvising with it, using your knowledge of keys and scales but also relying on your ear. The following page contains a solo played over this progression.

72. **Fantasy in Rhythm**  C. Soole

Here is a solo played over Rhythm Changes with substitutions at various points. On the recording it is played fast (mm ♩=220), but learn it slowly at first. Once you learn a phrase, make up your own variations on it as well as improvising over the Rhythm Changes demo.

BLUES CHANGES

You have already learnt many Blues melodies played over several variations on the 12 bar Blues progression. Shown below is the most basic form of 12 bar Blues in the **key of C**. This type of soloing works well with a Chicago, Texas or Jump Blues band. In these musical situations, scale substitutions and outside playing are generally undesirable and detract from the music. The most important thing when playing with any band is to use your ears and play what is appropriate to the context.

73.   Blues Changes (1)   P. Gelling

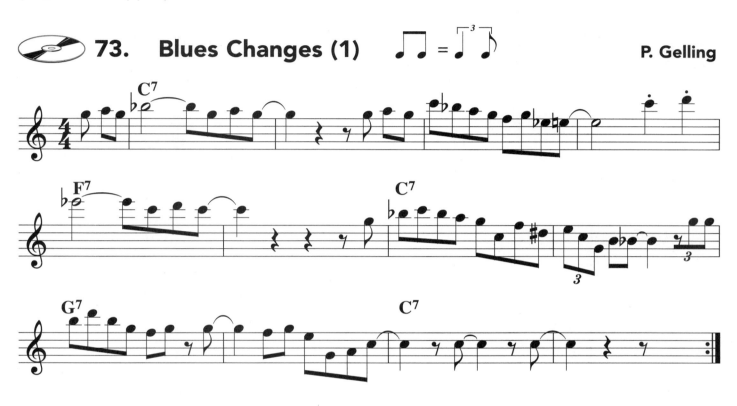

Here is a similar set of Blues changes with a few more chords. Again, this is straight Blues rather than Jazz Blues, so the lines come from Dominant 7th arpeggios and the Blues scale.

74.   Blues Changes (2)   P. Gelling

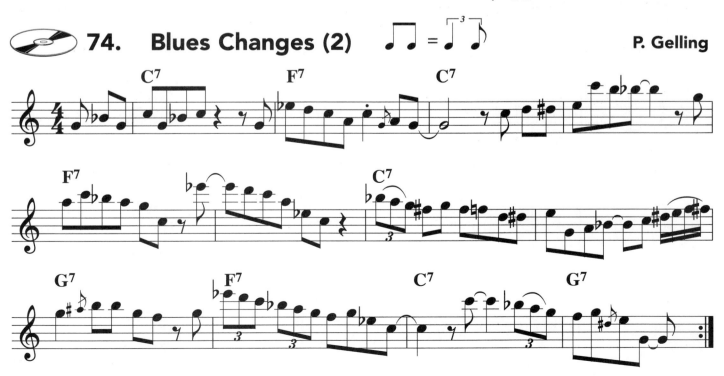

BLUES CHANGES USING SUBSTITUTIONS

When you play a Blues with a Jazz band, there are likely to be substitutions used, particularly over the last four bars of the form. The following example demonstrates a standard Jazz Blues type of solo. Notice the use of diminished and minor 7th chords along with the dominants.

75.   Blues Changes (3)   P. Gelling

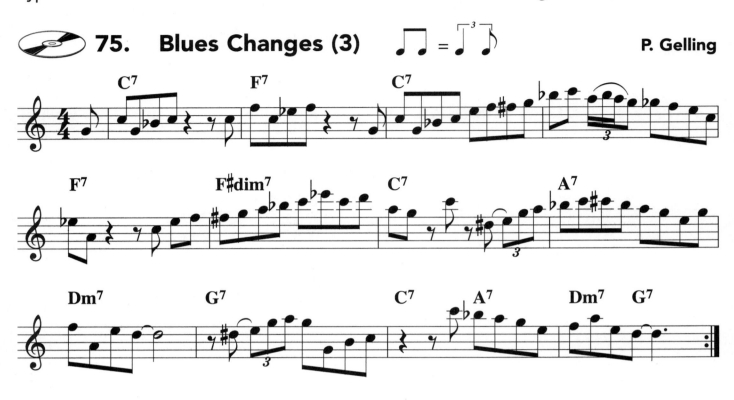

The next example is a more complex Bebop style blues. It contains many more chords and a different style of phrasing. Once again, learn it and then use the ideas to make up your own lines. It is also essential to listen to albums for the way various players approach the Blues. This form of music is likely to be used at any jam session, so learn it well.

76.   Blues Changes (4)   P. Gelling

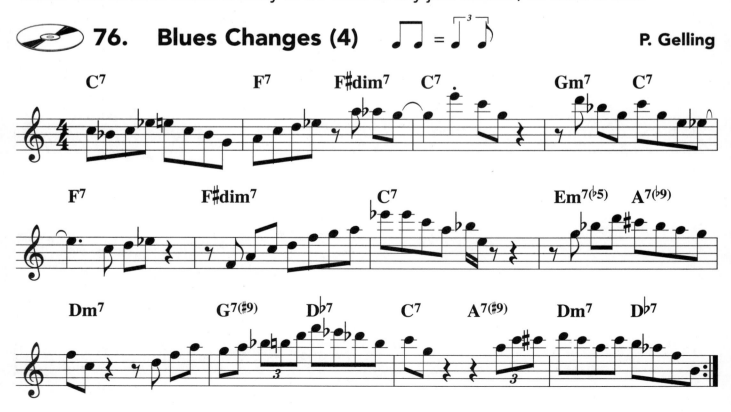

LISTENING

Apart from books, your most important source of information as a musician will be recordings. Listen to albums which feature sax players. Some important styles and players to look out for are: **R&B, Soul, Funk** – Maceo Parker and Pee Wee Ellis (Solo or with James Brown) Candy Dulfer, King Curtis, Junior Walker and Fathead Newman. **Blues, Jazz, Rock** – A.C. Reed, Eddie Shaw, Eddie "Cleanhead" Vinson, David Sanborn, Scott Page, Michael Brecker and Tom Scott. **Jazz** – Charlie Parker, Lester Young, Coleman Hawkins, Sidney Bechet, John Coltrane, Wayne Shorter, Sonny Rollins, Sonny Stitt, Art Pepper, Paul Desmond, Stan Getz, Dexter Gordon, Illinois Jacquet, Stanley Turrentine, Eddie Harris, Ben Webster, Johnny Hodges, Roland Kirk, Ornette Coleman, Albert Ayler, Steve Coleman and Chris Potter.

When you are listening to albums, try to sing along with the solos and imagine the fingerings and techniques you would use to achieve the sounds you are hearing. This helps you absorb the music and before long, it starts to come out in your own playing. It is also valuable to play along with albums, sometimes imitating what you are hearing and other times improvising. This is very good ear training and is also a lot of fun.

TRANSCRIBING

As well as playing along with albums and imitating what you hear, it is important to work out solos and melodies you admire exactly and write them down. This is called **transcribing**. By doing this, you can analyse the player's note choices and rhythmic idiosyncrasies and find out exactly what makes them sound the way they do. By doing this, you will be able to analyze the lines to understand what it is you like about them and then incorporate them into your own playing. It is important to transcribe a variety of players from different eras rather than just imitating one favorite (who wants to be a clone?). You will learn something different from each player and will also open yourself up to new ideas and new sounds. All the great players have done lots of transcribing. Make it part of your daily practice routine. When you have memorized a new melody or solo, try playing it with a play along recording of the song it came from or one with a similar progression (e.g. a Blues, or Rhythm Changes). Once you can play the solo perfectly, use it as a basis for improvising and then use the ideas you come up with next time you play with other musicians. Make a habit of this and your playing will never stop developing.

For more books and recordings by Peter Gelling, visit: **www.bentnotes.com**

SERVING THE SONG

It is important to remember that scales, arpeggios and techniques are just the tools for making music. What moves people most is the emotion in music. When you are playing a song, everything you play should help communicate the meaning and emotion of the composition itself. The great tenor saxophonist Lester Young once said he would never improvise on a song he didn't know the words to. Listen to singers and the way they express the lyrics and the melody. When you hear a great sax player (or any great instrumentalist) it is almost as if they are singing through their instrument. The following solo uses a vocal style and uses many expressions which are not written on the page. Listen carefully to the recording and try to get all these expressions into your playing. The next step is to add these expressions to your own improvising. Keep practicing, keep playing and have fun.

77. Angelica   C. Soole

209

INDEX OF FINGERINGS

To play the higher note, add the octave key.

To play the higher note, add the octave key.

E

To play the higher note, add the octave key.

F

To play the higher note, add the octave key.

F♯ or **G♭**

To play the higher note, add the octave key.

G

To play the higher note, add the octave key.

G♯ or **A♭**

To play the higher note, add the octave key.

A

To play the higher note, add the octave key.

212

A♯ or **B♭**

To play the higher note, add the octave key.

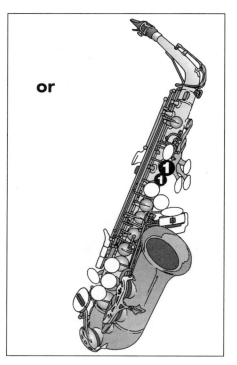

or

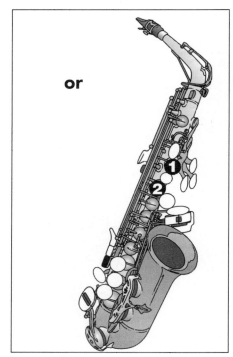

or

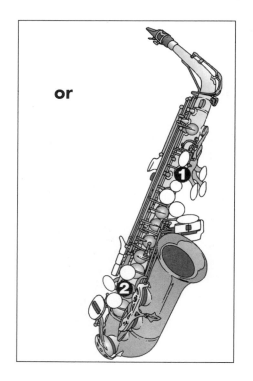

or

B

To play the higher note, add the octave key.

C

To play the higher note, add the octave key.

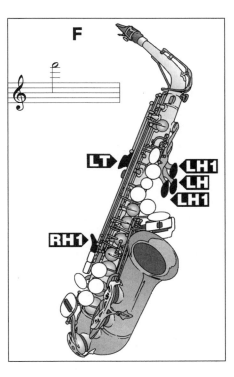

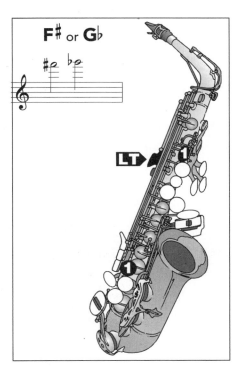

ALTERED CHORDS CHART

The chord chart below features chords which have one or more alterations to one of the given formulas, and are therefore called **altered chords**, as described in lesson 46.

CHORD NAME	CHORD FORMULA	EXAMPLE	
Major Flat Fifth	1 3 ♭5	C♭5:	C E G♭
Minor Seventh Flat Fifth	1 ♭3 ♭5 ♭7	Cm7♭5:	C E♭ G♭ B♭
Seventh Sharp Fifth	1 3 ♯5 ♭7	C7♯5:	C E G♯ B♭
Seventh Flat Fifth	1 3 ♭5 ♭7	C7♭5:	C E G♭ B♭
Seventh Sharp Ninth	1 3 5 ♭7 ♯9	C7♯9:	C E G B♭ D♯
Seventh Flat Ninth	1 3 5 ♭7 ♭9	C7♭9:	C E G B♭ D♭
Seventh Sharp Fifth Flat Ninth	1 3 ♯5 ♭7 ♭9	C7♯5♭9:	C E G♯ B♭ D♭
Ninth Sharp Fifth	1 3 ♯5 ♭7 9	C9♯5:	C E G♯ B♭ D
Ninth Flat Fifth	1 3 ♭5 ♭7 9	C9♭5:	C E G♭ B♭ D
Ninth Sharp Eleventh	1 3 5 ♭7 9 ♯11	C9♯11:	C E G B♭ D F♯
Minor Ninth Major Seventh	1 ♭3 5 7 9	Cm9(maj7):	C E♭ G B D
Thirteenth Flat Ninth	1 3 5 ♭7 ♭9 11* 13	C13:	C E G B♭ D♭ F* A
Thirteenth Flat Five Flat Ninth	1 3 ♭5 ♭7 ♭9 11* 13	C13♭5♭9:	C E G♭ B♭ D♭ F* A

In altered chords, the notes to be altered are always written as part of the chord name, enabling you to construct the chord. For example, a **Cm7♯5♭9** (not listed above) is a **Cm7** chord with the fifth sharpened (**♯5**) and the ninth flattened (**♭9**). When you are working out a suitable shape for this chord, remember that the root note and/or the fifth note may be omitted.

Another type of alteration occurs when chord symbols are written thus:

Example 1: **G/F♯** bass
> This indicates that a **G** chord is played, but using an F♯ note in the bass.

Example 2: **C/G** bass
> This indicates a **C** chord with a **G** bass note.

Sometimes the word 'bass' will not be written (i.e. the symbol will be just G/F♯), but the same meaning is implied. These chords are often referred to as **slash chords**.

GLOSSARY OF MUSICAL TERMS

Accidental — a sign used to show a temporary change in pitch of a note (i.e. sharp ♯ , flat ♭ , double sharp **✗** , double flat ♭♭ , or natural ♮). The sharps or flats in a key signature are not regarded as accidentals.

Ad lib — to be played at the performer's own discretion.

Anacrusis — a note or notes occurring before the first bar of music (also called 'lead-in' notes).

Arpeggio — the playing of a chord in single note fashion.

Bar — a division of music occurring between two bar lines (also called a 'measure').

Bar line — a vertical line drawn across the staff which divides the music into equal sections called bars.

Chord — a combination of three or more different notes played together.

Chord progression — a series of chords played as a musical unit (e.g. as in a song).

Chromatic scale — a scale ascending and descending in semitones.
e.g. **C** chromatic scale:

ascending: C C♯ D D♯ E F F♯ G G♯ A A♯ B C

descending: C B B♭ A A♭ G G♭ F E E♭ D D♭ C

Common time — and indication of ⁴⁄₄ time — four quarter note beats per bar (also indicated by **C**)

D.C al fine — a repeat from the sign (indicated thus 𝄋) to the word 'fine

Duration — the time value of each note.

Dynamics — the varying degrees of softness (indicated by the term 'piano') and loudness (indicated by the term 'forte') in music.

Eighth note — a note with the value of half a beat in ⁴⁄₄ time, indicated thus ♪ (also called a quaver).

Eighth rest — indicating half a beat of silence is written: ♩

Enharmonic — describes the difference in notation, but not in pitch, of two notes: e.g.

F♯ or G♭

First and second endings — signs used where two different endings occur. On the first time through ending one is played (indicated by the bracket |1̄‾‾‾‾|); then the progression is repeated and ending two is played (indicated |2̄‾‾‾).

Harmony — the simultaneous sounding of two or more different notes.

Improvise — to perform spontaneously; i.e. not from memory or from a written copy.

Interval — the distance between any two notes of different pitches.

Key — describes the notes used in a composition in regards to the major or minor scale from which they are taken; e.g. a piece 'in the key of C major' describes the melody, chords, etc., as predominantly consisting of the notes, **C, D, E, F, G, A,** and **B** — i.e. from the **C** scale.

Key signature — a sign, placed at the beginning of each stave of music, directly after the clef, to indicate the key of a piece. The sign consists of a certain number of sharps or flats, which represent the sharps or flats found in the scale of the piece's key. e.g.

 indicates a scale with **F♯** and **C♯** , which is **D** major; **D E F♯ G A B C♯ D.**
Therefore the key is **D** major.

Lead-In — same as anacrusis (also called a pick-up).

Leger lines — small horizontal lines upon which notes are written when their pitch is either above or below the range of the staff, e.g.

Legato — smoothly, well connected.

Major scale — a series of eight notes in alphabetical order based on the interval sequence tone - tone - semitone - tone - tone - tone - semitone, giving the familiar sound **do re mi fa so la ti do**.

Melody — a succession of notes of varying pitch and duration, and having a recognizable musical shape.

Metronome — a device which indicates the number of beats per minute, and which can be adjusted in accordance to the desired tempo.

e.g. **MM** (Maelzel Metronome) ♩ = 60 — indicates 60 quarter note beats per minute.

Natural — a sign (♮) used to cancel our the effect of a sharp or flat. The word is also used to describe the notes **A**, **B**, **C**, **D**, **E**, **F** and **G**; e.g. 'the natural notes'.

Octave — the distance between any given note with a set frequency, and another note with exactly double that frequency. Both notes will have the same letter name;

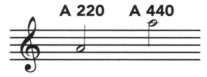

Pitch — the sound produced by a note, determined by the frequency of the string vibrations. The pitch relates to a note being referred to as 'high' or 'low'.

Repeat signs — in music, used to indicate a repeat of a section of music, by means of two dots placed before a double bar line:

In chord progressions, a repeat sign ⅟. , indicates and exact repeat of the previous bar.

Semitone — the smallest interval used in conventional music.

Sharp — a sign (♯) used to raise the pitch of a note by one semitone.

Staccato — to play short and detached. Indicated by a dot placed above the note:

Staff — five parallel lines together with four spaces, upon which music is written.

Syncopation — displacing the normal flow of accents in music. Usually from on the beat to off the beat.

Tempo — the speed of a piece.

Tie — a curved line joining two or more notes of the same pitch, where the second note(s) is not played, but its time value is added to that of the first note.

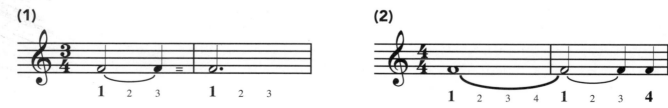

Timbre — a quality which distinguishes a note produced on one instrument from the same note produced on any other instrument (also called 'tone colour'). A given note on the guitar will sound different (and therefore distinguishable) from the same pitched note on piano, violin, flute etc.

Transposition — the process of changing music from one key to another.